Forex Trading For Beginners:

The Best Techniques to Financial Freedom for A Living and Work From Home Using Simple Strategies, High Probability Method, Psychology For Forex Market bases, In The Zone

ROBERT ZONE

Table of Contents

Introduction

Chapter 1   **How to Start Forex Trading**

Chapter 2   **Technical and Fundamental Analysis**

Chapter 3   **Forex Trading Strategies**

Chapter 4   **Choosing A Broker**

Chapter 5   **Forex Market**

Chapter 6   **Forex Trading Psychology**

Chapter 7   **Money Mistake to avoid**

Chapter 8   **Trading the Breakout**

Chapter 9   **Systems and Techniques for Beginners**

Conclusion

© **Copyright 2019 - All rights reserved.**

The content contained within this book may not be reproduced, duplicated or transmitted without direct written permission from the author or the publisher.

Under no circumstances will any blame or legal responsibility be held against the publisher, or author, for any damages, reparation, or monetary loss due to the information contained within this book. Either directly or indirectly.

Legal Notice:

This book is copyright protected. This book is only for personal use. You cannot amend, distribute, sell, use, quote or paraphrase any part, or the content within this book, without the consent of the author or publisher.

Disclaimer Notice:

Please note the information contained within this document is for educational and entertainment purposes only. All effort has been executed to present accurate, up to date, and reliable, complete information. No warranties of any kind are declared or implied. Readers acknowledge that the author is not engaging in the rendering of legal, financial, medical or professional advice. The content within this book has been derived from various sources. Please consult a licensed professional before attempting any techniques outlined in this book.

By reading this document, the reader agrees that under no circumstances is the author responsible for any losses, direct or indirect, which are incurred as a result of the use of information contained within this document, including, but not limited to, — errors, omissions, or inaccuracies.

Introduction

The most important thing to take note before starting your Forex trading journey is that this particular endeavor is not a get-rich-quick scheme. Do not expect to make a lot of money doing this for a living. Unless, of course, you are handling large amounts of money, such as those who handle hedge funds and fund managers. However, even then there are a lot of risks involved, and some people with large capitals can lose a huge amount in the Forex market. With a correct system and of course some luck, traders can make a decent and steady profit from the Forex market. A reasonably successful trader can expect to make a monthly return of around 1 or 2 percent of his or her capital. This may also result in around a 25 percent return annually. Of course, this will only happen if the market conditions are favorable and there are no other unforeseen circumstances, such as war, political upheaval, large natural disasters, and other events that will occur.

Using these figures, a person who invests around US$100,000 in the Forex market can expect an annual return of around US$25,000. This is definitely a good chunk of change, but most will likely not want to make Forex trading a full-time job. Recent data has also shown that only a quarter, or 25 percent, of traders in retail Forex end up earning any profit in three months. A good chunk of these traders are day traders, while the rest only take a small number of positions and hold them for longer periods.

Currency pairs will more often than not only move by minuscule amounts throughout a few days. These pairs typically rise and fall by around 10 percent over a year. Some people view the Forex market as a form of gambling. However, traders would argue that the odds in Forex are much higher than any casino game out there. This form of analyzed betting gives traders a big advantage as they have a lot of clues and data to go on to make informed decisions. It has to be noted that similar to traditional gambling, people may experience a string of bad bets. No matter what method you follow or how strict you are with your analysis and trading, there will be some days where you just can't win. On average, one out of three trades will be a losing trade. In reality, this could be much worse depending on how lucky you are.

Then again, if you work hard, and focus on your strategies and charts, it is possible to make a modest amount of money in the Forex market. Now that I have given the clear picture of Forex expectations one must understand that it is possible to become a successful trader if you are truly dedicated to it. If you think Forex expectation is the problem, then, you must find solutions to overcome the expectations that aren't healthy to your trading journey. Let us dig deeper into the concept of managing expectations in Forex trading.

Do you know why it is important to manage Forex expectations? Well, as I mentioned if you are not aware of Forex expectations, you'll become one of those traders who quit even before beginning the trading journey. Hence, you must try to manage your Forex expectations. First of all, what are the expectations? Let's be honest, and it is impossible to set aside expectations because everything in this world is based on expectations. Even the most successful Forex trader would have entered the market with some expectations. However, the important point is related to the way you handled the market expectations. If you let your expectations play the game, then, you are not going to win the game. Hence, setting reasonable expectations is crucial. You must consider the factors that will impact your expectations so that you can get a clear view of it.

Emotion is the triggering factor that controls your expectations. When you set reasonable expectations, and when you get the opportunity to meet them, it feels great, right? But then, how does this relate to trading? Basically, human beings are born with the ability to avoid pain. We have it in our body. But, your pain-avoidance ability works differently in trading that it links with emotions. When you set a trading expectation, you try to avoid all the information that invalidates your expectation. Somehow, you find reasons, rationalize, and even worse, you make yourself feel great about avoiding the information. This isn't healthy. You might end up blowing your trading account as a whole, so think about this!

If you have been to a foreign country, you know that you cannot buy your favorite food and drinks in the country you are visiting with your home country's currency. To avoid such a predicament, individuals have the option to convert their money into the currency of the country they are visiting at the airport.

In addition, you may have received some payment for services in a foreign currency, and you needed to exchange the money into your country's currency for you to use it. Regardless of the situations you had interacting with foreign currency. It is likely highly you have participated in forex in one way or another. A person can participate in Forex Trading whether he or she is traveling to a foreign country, or doing business in his or her country.

What Is Forex Trading

The word 'forex' is short for 'foreign exchange.' It involves the process of converting one currency into another currency for reasons including tourism, trading, and business.

Although a person can participate in foreign exchange by traveling to a different country and exchanging his or her currency for the foreign country's currency, the foreign exchange market is more significant than that. The foreign exchange market is a global forum for exchanging substantial national currencies against each other.

Due to the international spread of finance and trade, the forex markets experience high demands for foreign currencies, which makes the market the most significant money market in the world.

When multinational companies intend to buy goods from other countries, companies need to find the local currency first. That exchange will involve vast amounts of currency exchange. As a result, the local currency value will move up as the demand for that currency increases. With that exchanging going on around the world, the exchange rate always changes.

When global traders exchange currencies, currencies have a specific exchange rate, the price of currency changes according to the law of supply and demand; the higher the demand, the higher the supply and the higher the exchange rate.

The foreign trading market has no centralized marketplace for foreign exchange. Foreign exchange bureaus operate electronically through computer networks between traders all over the world.

Therefore, foreign trading goes on for 24 hours a day, six days a week in leading financial centers of major capital cities around the world. Investment and commercial banks carry out most of the Forex Trading in the international marketplaces in place of clients and investors.

Principles of Forex Trading

1. Learn the Market's Trends

It is essential for one to be able to predict the changing nature of the foreign exchange market in order to be successful in Forex Trading.

Accordingly, a person should understand the general direction of the marketplace. Trends can be uptrend, downtrend, or sideways trend. Identifying a pattern can profit a person in that he or she will be able to trade with the trend.

Uptrends are trends that move upwards, indicating an appreciation in currency value. Downtrends move downwards as an indication of depreciation in currency value. Sideways trends show that the currencies are neither appreciating nor depreciating.

2. Stay Focused and Control Your Emotions

Forex Trading is a challenging marketplace that can cause a person to lose confidence and to give up in the toughest of times. That is understandable given that traders put in their hard-earned money.

As a result, when a person experiences loss, he or she can lose focus when negative emotions become overwhelming. Some of the negative emotions a person may experience include panic, frustration, depression, and desperation.

It is, therefore, essential for one to become aware of the negative emotions that result from Forex Trading so that he or she may minimize the emotional effects of loss and remain focused.

3.   Learn Risk Mitigation Tactics

In order to achieve the profits that a person anticipates, the person needs to minimize the likelihood of financial loss.

Since the forex market keeps on changing, the risks, therefore, keep on changing. The most crucial risk management rule is that a person should not risk more than he or she can afford to lose. Traders who are willing to invest more than they make, become very susceptible to Forex Trading risks.

Consequently, a person can mitigate potential losses by placing stop-loss orders, exchanging more than one currency pair, using software programs for help, and limiting the use of financial leverage.

4.   Establish Personal Forex Trading Limits

A person should know when to stop Forex Trading. One can stop Forex Trading when he or she has an unproductive trading plan, or when he or she is continually experiencing losses.

An ineffective Forex Trading plan may not bring trade to an end, but it will not function as well as a trader may expect. In that case, the trader can consider stopping the trade, constantly changing markets, and the decreasing volatility within a particular foreign trading tool may also cause a trader to take a break from Forex Trading.

In addition, when a person is not in a good physical or emotional state, he or she may want to think about taking a break to deal with personal issues.

5.   Use Technology to Your Benefit

Being up-to-date with existing technological developments can be gratifying in Forex Trading.

Given that forex markets utilize the online forum, high-speed internet connections can increase Forex Trading performance significantly. In order to make the most of Forex Trading, a person must take it as a full-time occupation, and he or she must embrace new technologies. Similarly, receiving forex market current information with smartphones makes it possible for forex traders to track trades anywhere.

Forex Trading is an aggressive enterprise that needs a trader to have an equally competitive edge. Therefore, a forex trader needs to maximize his or her business's potential by taking full advantage of the available technology.

6. Make Use of a Forex Trading Plan

A Forex Trading plan comprises of rules and guidelines that stipulate a forex trader's entry, exit, and money management principles.

A trading plan provides the opportunity for a forex trader to try out a Forex Trading idea before the trader risks real money. In so doing, a trader can access historical information that helps to know whether a Forex Trading plan is feasible and what outcomes he or she can expect.

When a forex trader comes up with a Forex Trading plan that shows potentially favorable outcomes, he or she can use the trading plan in real Forex Trading situations. The idea is for the forex trader to adhere to the trading plan.

Buying or selling currencies outside of the Forex Trading plans, even if a trader makes a profit, is poor trading, which can end any expectation the plan may have had.

Different Types of Forex Traders

Because foreign markets become flooded with the constant demand for currency exchange, four types of currency traders facilitate the smooth operation of forex markets.

1.   Scalpers

Forex scalpers are dealers who buy or sell currencies, hold on to the exchanged currencies, and then wait for them to have higher and favorable exchange rates before the dealers can change their new currencies back to their original versions.

The scalpers hold deals for seconds to minutes and open and close several positions within a single day. In other words, scalpers go in and out of positions several times each day.

Scalpers trade currencies based on real-time analysis. Scalpers aim to make a profit by selling or buying currencies and holding on to them for a short time before buying or selling the currencies back to the forex market for small gains.

Therefore, that means that scalpers should love sitting in front of their laptops or computers for the entire forex session without taking their eyes off the screen.

Scalping is widespread moments after essential data releases and interest rate announcements. That is because high-impact reports generate significant price moves within a short period.

However, while profits can accrue rapidly with profitable trades, huge losses can also accumulate if the scalper is using a faulty system or if the trader does not understand what he or she is doing.

2. Day Traders

Forex day traders control trading positions during each trading day. Day traders close the trading positions at the end of the trading day and ensure that there are no positions that remain open during the night.

Forex day traders use currency day trading systems that regulate whether to buy or sell a currency pair in the foreign exchange market. A currency pair is the quotation of two different currencies where the trader quotes the value of one currency in comparison to the other.

Day traders target day currencies that are very liquid to leverage their capital as soon as investment prices change in favorable directions. The traders pick a price position at the start of the day, act on their assessments, and finish the trading day with either a profit or a loss.

Forex day traders avoid holding positions overnight because that may result in stock price gaps, a consequence, which can be very costly.

3. Swing Traders

Swing traders take hold of a position over a few days to several weeks. They hold places for more than one trading session, although not longer than several weeks or a couple of months.

Swing traders aim to capture huge potential price moves. Some swing traders may look for volatile stocks with constant movements, whereas others prefer stock prices that are more predictable.

Swing traders have exposure to overnight and weekend risks, where prices could rift and open the following forex session with markedly different rates. However, swing traders can generate profit by using established risk or reward strategies that will help them to determine where they will enter assets, where they will place stop-loss orders, and to know where they can make profits. Stop-loss orders help to limit the loss when stock prices fall.

Swing traders come up with plans and strategies that will give them an advantage over may trades. The traders do that by looking for trade arrangements that facilitate predictable price movements in the price of the asset. However, no trade arrangement works every time.

4. Position Traders

Position traders hold on to investment positions for long periods, anticipating the investments to appreciate. The periods can extend from weeks to months. In that regard, position traders are less concerned with short-term changes in price movements.

Position traders follow trends, believing that once a pattern starts, it is likely to continue. As such, position traders incline toward obtaining the bulk of a trend's move, which would generate profit in their investment capital.

Position traders use both fundamental and technical analysis to help in making trading decisions. They also depend on macroeconomic influences, old trends, and overall market movements to get to their anticipated end.

For a trader to have success in position trading, the trader has to know the entry or exit points and have a strategy to mitigate risk mainly by placing stop-loss orders.

Advantage of Forex Trading

1.   Easy to Modify

Forex Trading markets put no restrictions on how much money a forex trader can use. Forex traders can trade a variety of goods and services.

In addition, the forex market does not have many rules and regulations for the forex trader to follow. The regulations that exist guide forex traders on when to enter and when to exit a trade.

2.   Individual Control

Nobody controls the foreign market. Therefore, a forex trader has complete autonomy concerning making a trade. The forex market regulates itself and levels the playing field.

There are no intermediaries involved – a forex trader trades directly in the open forex market, and a retail forex broker eases that process.

3.   Lucidity of Information

The Forex Trading market gives information straightforwardly to the public about the rates and price movement forecasts. The forex market traders have free and equal access to the market's information, and that makes it easy for the traders to make calculated and risk-free trading decisions.

Forex traders also have access to past information that helps in analyzing the market tendencies and forecasting the direction, which the market will take.

4.   Widespread Options

The forex market provides a variety of options to forex investors. As a result, forex investors can take advantage of the available options to trade in different currencies in pairs.

An investor has the option of getting into foreign exchange spot trade or trading in currency futures to make the most of his or her investment.

5. High Liquidity and Volume

The forex market trades in large amounts of currencies at any given time because of how active the foreign exchange is. Therefore, there are high chances for forex traders to trade currency pairs on demand.

Under normal market conditions, a forex trader can buy and sell quickly with the anticipation that there will be another forex trader on the other end who is willing to trade back.

6. Money-Making Gains

The forex market provides Forex Trading measures that guard against financial loss. To ensure that a forex trader maximizes of gaining profits, the forex market has provisions for minimizing loss through making stop-loss orders.

Stop-loss orders enable forex traders to determine the closing price of their trade and thereby avoiding unforeseen losses.

7. 24-Hour Market

Foreign exchange markets remain open for 24-hours a day and 6 days a week. That means that the market stays open most of the time, and it is not subject to external factors that may affect it.

Consequently, forex traders are flexible to work during the hours that suit them best.

8. Low Operation Costs

Operation costs in the forex currency markets are competent in trading in the forex market. The cost of operation in the currency market is in the form of spreads measured in pips. A pip is the fourth place after the decimal point of a percent.

For example, is the selling price was 2.5887, and the buying price was 2.5889, then the transaction cost is 2pips. Brokers may charge commissions on a fraction of the amount of the trade.

9. Chief Financial Market

The forex market is the biggest financial market in the world. That is because global corporations and big financial institutions participate dynamically in the foreign exchange market.

The foreign exchange market empowers major financial institutions to retail stockholders to seek out profits from currency variations connected to the global economy.

10. One Can Use the Leverage

The forex markets allow forex traders to capitalize on the advantage. Leveraging enables forex traders to be able to open positions for thousands of dollars while investing small amounts of money.

For example, when a forex trader trades at 40:1 leverage, he or she can trade $40 for every $1 that was in his or her account. That means that the forex trader can manage a trade of $40,000 for every $1,000 of investment.

Why Forex

The foreign exchange market is open to all types of traders, and it is more accessible than any other online trading platform in the world. Similarly, one can start trading with as little as $100. Therefore, foreign exchange markets have lower exchange capital prerequisites compared to other financial markets. A person can quickly sign up to open their trading account online, where most forex retail brokers operate.

Forex Trading is easy to learn, although it may be challenging to master. However, once an investor understands how the forex market works, he or she will be open to a world of vast opportunities that include becoming a foreign exchange account manager. A foreign exchange account manager can accumulate profits from trading as well as earning commissions for managing the Forex Trading accounts.

Foreign exchange markets make provisions for forex brokers to develop considerable trading volumes because of the leverage that the forex markets offer. That explains why forex traded get rewards like deposit bonuses when creating a Forex Trading account. Likewise, forex brokers give several incentives and promotions to financial institutions that enter Forex Trading. As a result, the forex market becomes a stimulating marketplace for Forex Trading.

Forex traders form international social communities as more people sign up every day. The social networks help forex investors to encounter an entire community of foreign exchange traders, thus making the forex market an interactive market to trade. In addition, forex traders can find many international forex experts, contributors, critics, and educators, among other members, in every conceivable language.

Moreover, forex traders can buy and sell risk-free, using a demonstration trading account. The account prevents traders from putting their investment at risk, and the traders can, therefore, move to the live forex markets whenever they please. The trading accounts enable forex traders to have access to real-time market information and the latest trading wisdom from foreign experts.

The forex market infrastructure is sophisticated, causing the performance of traders to be even more level. The forex market also has low spreads and commissions, thus making the transaction costs relatively small as a result. Besides, the foreign exchange market educates forex traders on global events, as the traders continue to trade online. Favorable trading conditions are crucial for foreign exchange traders.

Heavy security measures guard the foreign exchange markets, and several authorities control every forex broker. The bodies exist to make sure that forex traders have a safe space to carry out Forex Trading activities. However, forex traders are only with regulated brokers. Therefore, one must conduct a background check on available brokers in order to ensure that he or she works with the regulated brokers.

Online Forex Trading makes use of advanced trading software that generates regular updates that help forex investors to make real-time Forex Trading decisions. Consequently, Forex Trading becomes a rewarding way to buy and sell online, also due to third-party software developers who provide add-ons and plugins for popular trading platforms.

Finally, the forex markets allow traders to buy low and sell high. What's more, forex traders can trade assets without owning them, a practice that is called short selling. Furthermore, the use of leverage enables Forex traders to buy or sell more substantial amounts than what they have in their deposits.

Chapter 1 How to Start Forex Trading

Forex trading is not a trade that one can pull off without breaking a sweat before exchanging currencies. There has to be prior preparation, studies done and analyzation of the market patterns to make the first trade. Below is discussed the steps that a trader has to make so as to start trading forexes and be successful while doing so.

Forex Trading Terminology

There are a lot of terms used that are new to a trader who is just starting off and are vocabularies to them. It would do well to an aspiring trader to acquaint themselves with the new terms and understand the meaning behind them and how to use them appropriately when trading. This will prove essential to avoid miscomprehension of certain concepts when trading. To new traders, the terms may be a little bit difficult and also have a completely different meaning than the expected one from its word-formation. The following words discussed below are some of the new vocabularies that will be encountered by a new trader, which are common in the language of trading.

A pip. A pip is the lowest measure of the value of movement of currency under observation. The term pip is, however, an abbreviation of the term- percentage in point. A pip, as the lowest measurable value of the movement that the currency makes, always measures ad 1% of the currency that a trader wants to exchange. When in the forex market a currency increases or decreases by a single pip, the inference has the meaning that the currency either increased or decreased by 1%. A great example is when the market analysis tools show that the US dollar has increased by a pip. This is to mean that the US dollar has increased in its value by $0.0001.

That is how a pip is inferred and it's meaning. Trade is always made in terms of pips, and a trader can make trades with many pips as possible. This is because the pips are the lowest value that is measured by the currency.

The base currency. The base currency is the type of currency that a trader has and is currently holding. The base currency is likely the currency of the country that you're from. If a trader is from the US, his or her base currency will be the US dollar. If the trader is from the UK, the base currency of the trader will be the pound. The base currencies of traders therefore different across many traders around the globe due to different geographical differences.

The asking price. The asking price is a term that is used to refer to the amount of money that your broker firm will demand from or will ask from you when you are making a trade. A broker always demands this price, or this amount of money when they are accepting the pair of currencies to be traded from you. The price id for buying the quote that you've made of the pair of currencies. A note to be made is that the asking price; made by the brokerage firms, is always higher than the bid price, as will be discussed immediately below.

Bid price. The bid price is mostly used in reference to the brokerage firms, where it is the amount of money that the brokers will be willing to buy or to bid the base currency that you are currently holding. The broker firm sets the bid price according to their ability to bid on the base currency that has.

Quote currency. The quote currency, unlike the base currency, is the currency that a trader wants and is willing to purchase, in exchange for his or her base currency. If a trader wants to exchange US dollars to get South African Rand, the currency of South Africa; the Rand is the quote currency. It is always stroked against the base currency when trading and when the currencies are made into pairs.

The spread. This is the commission that the broker firm receives from being a platform where forex trading can take place. When referred to, the spread means the difference in value between the bid price made by the broker and the asking price, also quoted by the broker.

These are but a few but the major terms that are used in the forex trading world. Knowing this alone will not be enough, you have to be familiar with more words and phrases that can be found in books concerning forex trading. Not only in books but also videos, forums and such where forex trading is discussed.

Finding the Right Broker Firm

So as to trade forex, you will have to have a brokerage firm that will be an online platform from which you'll open and close trade. Finding the right broker firm is an important process for other brokers can be a sham out to cheat people of their money. It is therefore paramount that a trader carries out research on the available broker firms and picks out the best and one that is highly recommended for its services. When deciding on which broker firm to go with, look at the ask and the bid price that the broker quotes, and other important aspects including the margin and the leverage level that they offer. The customer service should also be top-notch for the broker, which will be great for a trader who is just starting off. Most of the broker companies also offer studies on how to carry out forex trading and those come in handy to the new traders. Reviews by other forex traders is a great place to start on choosing the quality of a broker.

Making an Analysis of the Worldwide Economy

To make gains and profits and gains in trades that you are going to make, analyzing the economic trends of the worldwide economy is of great import to be fully aware of the factors that may trigger the currencies to increase or decrease in value. This is important in making a correct prediction on the pair of currencies you're exchanging, whether they will make a profit or a loss. Factors that are important to look into when evaluating the global economy are like the political climate of countries whose currencies have a strong value, natural factors that may influence the economy of countries, the Gross Domestic Product of the country whose currency you want to exchange with your base currency, and other minor factors such as the investment rate of the said country. Evaluating which countries are looking up to growth and development opportunities is also important in determining the quote currency to use impairing up currencies to make a trade. Also on the analysis of the worldwide economy, when the currency of the country you seek to purchase in exchange of your base currency is doing well and is set to increase in its value, convert your base currency into the quote currency. On the other hand, convert the quote currency into the base currency in case its value increases. There are various online sites that have analysis tools on the economic performance of different countries that you may seek for them to be your quote currency. Others rank counties in terms of their GDP that makes it easier for you to choose the countries that are projected for growth and development. Being in touch with the trending news globally is a plus in getting information relevant to trading forex. A new forex trader may subscribe to a few forex trading channels and outlets to be constantly on toes of events and happenings that may trigger the value of currencies to either increase o decrease, which may result in the reversal of the outlook of the trade made. Having relevant information at all times is key in making gains and preventing the loss of your money and probably your account is cleared.

Opening the First Trade

Pairing currencies and making the first trade; opening and closing a trade happens when the quote currency to be paired by the base currency have been paired and there is an opportune trading window. Opening a trade is making an order to purchase a certain currency and in exchange for your base current through your broker firm. You'll have the analysis tools, that are commonly offered by the brokers in software programs. The execution of making an order in some platforms might be instant while in some other platforms, it might be a tad bit slower. Nonetheless, most brokerage firms offer live prices and values of the currencies that are to traded and their exchange rates and the instant changes to their values are displayed. The first trade for a new trader might just be one or others might open up new trades over a short period of time. It is advisable that just several enough trades be opened, which the new trader is comfortable and at ease in trading.

Chapter 2 Technical and Fundamental Analysis

After reviewing the strategies that are used in Forex trading, we will discuss the tools that are used in Forex trading. We are going to keep it relatively simple because frankly, it's not necessary to overcomplicate things. The main tools that we are going to focus on are tools that will help you keep track of pricing trends and help you find signals of trend reversals.

The first thing to consider is technical vs. fundamental analysis. If you are someone who has done trading on the stock market, you will have some idea of what these two concepts are about. In the Forex markets, there are some general similarities and some differences. When it comes to technical analysis, there are more similarities to be found than differences, however. Technical analysis involves the use of tools that can be applied to any financial instrument that is traded on a marketplace. The tools of technical analysis can be used to get information about trading volume, pricing trends, and pricing trend reversals. There are three main tools that are used by most traders. The first tool that is used is the candlestick charts. Candlestick charts divide up a graph of pricing of a financial asset into short time intervals, using a graphical representation (in the form of a "candlestick") that gives you pricing information for each time interval. The candlestick will let you know what the high and low prices were for the time interval, what the open and closing prices were for the time interval, and whether the closing price finished above or below the opening price, indicating whether traders were "bullish" or "bearish" on the financial asset for the given time period. Moreover, candlesticks help you see how trends are developing and possibly reversing. We are going to talk about candlesticks more in a bit.

The other tools that are frequently used include moving averages, which smooth out pricing data by averaging them, Bollinger bands, which help you see the one standard deviation pricing rage for a financial asset, and the relative strength indicator which helps you determine whether an asset is "overbought" or "oversold." You can also look at the average pip movement.

What technical analysis comes down to, is it's a set of tools that helps you determine the buildup of trends and pricing shifts as supply and demand for a given financial asset changes in the marketplace. Technical analysis is not concerned with what is causing those price movements, or even what the underlying financial security is.

Fundamental analysis is an entirely different ballgame.

Fundamental analysis for Forex markets is far broader, and actually quite a bit simpler. The main components of fundamental analysis when currencies are the subject of interest are the interest rate of the central bank, the interest rate of the central bank for the country that is the other party to a given currency pair (and so we are really considering the interest rate differential between the two countries), and the overall economic health of each country. For example, the exports that a country relies on are important, and therefore changes in commodity prices are something that needs to be considered. GDP growth rates, unemployment, and other factors are things to look at where fundamental analysis is concerned. If one member of a currency pair is performing in a much better way in comparison to the other when it comes to these metrics, that can mean that it is the better choice for the currency pair.

You want to look for both positive and negative news events, but a bad event can drive investors out of a country, such as a terrorist attack, or a political upheaval. It's important to keep up with the news even if such events seem unlikely in current circumstances; many quiet years can go by before the international situation deteriorates or becomes chaotic. A large-scale terrorist attack could hurt an economy or drive tourism away, at least temporarily. An economic recession can also cause problems if it is localized to one country.

- Factors to Consider in Technical Analysis
- Candlestick Charts

Now, let's turn our attention to the specifics of technical analysis. The first tool of technical analysis that a new trader needs to learn is candlestick charts. A candlestick is a representation of price movement over a specific time period that you set for your chart. For example, you can set the time period to a minute, 5 minutes, or even one day. This is the trading session. The candlestick will have a body, and two upper and lower shadows or wicks.

Image from Wikipedia, courtesy of Probe-meteo.com

The upper wick represents the high price for the trading session. The lower wick represents the low price for the candlestick. The body of the candlestick represents the opening and closing prices for the trading session. There are two general types of candlesticks. They can be bullish, in which case they represent a trading session where prices were pushed upward. In that case, the top of the candlestick body is the closing price for the trading session, while the bottom of the candlestick would be the opening price for the trading session. Bullish candlesticks are either solid green in color or outlined green on trading charts. If the chart is black and white, the candlestick will be an outline for the bullish trading session.

If the asset price dropped during the trading session, then you have a bearish candlestick. On charts with white backgrounds, they are colored red—and in most cases with charts, with black backgrounds. Bearish candlesticks are colored white—on a black-and-white chart. A bearish candlestick will have a solid black body. For a bearish candlestick, the top of the candlestick body represents the opening price for the trading session, while the bottom of the candlestick body is the closing price – so this represents a case where the price dropped. In both cases (bearish and bullish), the meaning of the wicks or shadows extended out from the candlesticks is the same.

GREEN:RED:

Image from Wikipedia, courtesy of Probe-meteo.com

The trader studies candlestick patterns in order to look for signals that trends are going to reverse. A candlestick pattern, by itself, is not a reason to enter or exit a trade. The trader will "confirm" the signal seen in the candlesticks with at least two other methods that we will discuss below.

Many trading platforms use black backgrounds for Forex charts. In this case, the white candlesticks are bearish, and the green outlined candlesticks are bullish.

There are many patterns that you need to become familiar with in order to be successful using candlestick charts to help you make the right trades. The first thing to look for is called an engulfing pattern. This happens when the candlestick of one type (bearish or bullish) is followed by a candlestick of the opposite type. The second candlestick will have a much larger body, indicating that the price was driven upwards by a large amount during the trading session. The candlestick would "engulf" or completely cover the previous candlestick. This type of pattern is shown below. It indicates a coming upward trend in price.

The next pattern that we are going to look at is called "three white soldiers." The name is historical and comes from the old black-and-white charts where the bullish candlesticks would be white with black outlines. Today we might call it "three green soldiers." This is three bullish candlesticks in a row, with higher highs in succession. This indicates a coming upward trend. This is shown below.

Next, we come to a "doji" indecision candle. This candle has a thin line for a body, indicating that the opening and closing prices for the trading session were the same. The candle will also have long wicks, indicating that the prices were pushed up high and down low during the trading session, but they ended up back at the opening price. This is the "indecision," traders were neither bullish or bearish during the trading session.

Another signal that an upward trend in price is coming is called an inverted hammer. In this case, you will see a bullish candlestick with a relatively narrow body, but with a long upward wick, indicating the prices were pushed up high during the trading session. Even though the high was not maintained, the price closed higher than the open, and the opening price is the low price for the trading session. It should be confirmed using technical indicators like a moving average crossover.

A hammer is this pattern in reverse, and if a hammer occurs at the top of an uptrend, this may indicate a coming downward trend in price.

There is also a pattern known as a shooting star. In this case, there is a bearish candle in the form of an inverted hammer, appearing at the top of an uptrend. So it will have a long wick shooting upward, the "shooting" part of the star, but it will close at a lower price than the open.

The same types of patterns that form with bullish candlesticks can form with bearish candlesticks as well. In these cases, they indicate a coming downward trend in prices. For example, we can have three bearish candlesticks in a row, indicating declining prices, with lower lows for each closing price. This is called three black crows, a historical reference to the time when the charts were black and white, and the bearish candlesticks were solid black in color.

Next, we consider an evening star. This is a pattern that can indicate a coming downtrend. When there is an evening star, you first see a large upward push in prices with a large bullish candlestick. This is followed by a hammer that is a bearish hammer, so the price closed below the open. That indicates that although the price had been pushed up, it wasn't possible to keep finding buyers.

The abandoned baby pattern appears at the end of a downtrend. In this case, there is a large bearish candle that ends a streak of bearish candles. Then, there is a doji indecision candle, indicating that sellers are not coming to the table anymore. This is followed by a bullish candle indicating a buying spree is coming up:

The terms bullish and bearish used with candlesticks come from the stock market, where rising prices are desirable. Keep in mind that on the Forex markets, rising or falling prices are not framed in the same way, because you might be betting on the secondary currency and so you are hoping for falling prices. So for the Forex markets, bullish means that the primary currency is rising against the secondary currency, while bearish means the secondary currency is rising against the primary currency. So whether something is really "bullish" or not depends on what side of the trade you are on.

There are many other candlestick patterns that you can use. An entire book could be written on this topic, and we don't have space to cover them all. But you should be educated on them all before you start trading, so you should look for videos, articles, and even Udemy courses about candlesticks online.

- Strength Indicators

Another technical indicator you may want to use is the relative strength indicator. This indicator helps you get an idea if a financial asset is overbought or oversold. This helps you determine the momentum in a trend. When we say an asset is overbought, this means that the price has been pushed too high with respect to the actual value of the asset. In other words, the price is pushed higher than the fundamentals would indicate is valid. When this happens, the price can continue increasing, but the momentum of the price increase is probably going to peter out, and the price trend will peak out and eventually reverse. At this point, in short order, people holding the asset are going to recognize that it's overpriced, and they will start dumping it on the market so they can exit their positions at a relative high pricing point.

This can happen on the downside as well. In this case, we are talking about an oversold asset. This means the price that is driven down lower than the fundamentals would indicate a valid price. At this point, momentum to push the price down is going to be decreasing, even if, for a while, prices continue to drop. This probably indicates that a trend reversal is coming, and prices will start rising again. It's just a matter of time before buyers recognize that the asset has now become available at a bargain price, and so they will start moving in to buy the asset and push prices back up.

The RSI runs over 0-100. There are different conventions used with the relative strength indicator, but the standard is using 70-80 as the cutoff point for overbought. That is, if the RSI is above 70 or 80 (70 is probably too conservative), you should consider a rising price trend as overbought, and it will probably reverse soon. For oversold conditions, and RSI less than 20 is typically used.

- Bollinger Bands

The next technical indicator that you should at least be aware of is called Bollinger bands. This is a more complicated indicator that brings three pieces of information together. It consists of three curves. In the center, there is a moving average curve. You can set the type of moving average that you want to use, but by default, it will be a simple moving average. There are curves above and below the moving average that show the one standard deviations above and below the moving average. This helps you to determine levels of support and resistance as well as signs that a breakout may occur.

During a timeframe that the financial asset is ranging, it will have price fluctuations that are contained within the Bollinger bands. Therefore, if you are buying a currency pair, you can wait for the price to drop to the lower Bollinger (or alternatively, you can buy when the price touches the moving average if there are other signs it will begin rising in price). Then, you sell when the price moves to the upper Bollinger band.

When the candlesticks move outside one of the outer Bollinger bands, this can be a sign of a coming breakout. If the wicks, or especially the body, go above the upper-level Bollinger band, this can be taken as an indicator that the price is going to start moving upward, until it establishes a new higher level of pricing support.

Alternatively, you can look for instances of the candlesticks going below the lower Bollinger band, which can indicate the possibility of a break to the downside in prices, which can be a start of a new downward trend.

- The Depth Line

You may also take a look at the market in-depth in order to determine the supply and demand for a given currency pair. This tells you the number of open buy-and-sell orders for the currency pair. The larger the number of buying and selling orders, the more the depth of the market. The importance of this value is the higher the depth line, the more liquidity there is in the market for the given currency pair. It will also give you an idea of how likely it is that your order will be filled in a timely fashion at a given price. Of course, for major currency pairs such as the EUR/USD, liquidity is never going to be an issue. However, even in that case, you can use market depth so that you can see how many open orders there are at different price points. There will be an ask volume and a bid volume. The ask is the asking price from sellers, and the bid is the price that buyers are bidding and willing to pay. You can also see the total ask less total bid on your charts so that you can get an estimate of how different these values are – giving an indication of how quickly orders are going to be filled. If there is a large difference in value between the bid and ask prices, then that can indicate that there is going to be some difficulty in filling orders. On the other hand, if the difference is small, orders will be filled quickly.

- Factors to Consider in Fundamental Analysis

In this section, we are going to briefly examine the main factors you should consider when using fundamental analysis as a part of your toolkit to determine which currencies you want to invest in.

- Interest Rates

Interest rates are an important metric to consider. There are many factors that will determine the strength of a currency, but all things considered equal, higher interest rates mean the currency is going to be more in demand, and therefore it will rise against other currencies. If the interest rate in the United States rises, outside investors will be more interested in buying bonds and other interest producing assets inside the United States, and they are going to need dollars to do it. Therefore, this means that the demand for dollars will rise, and prices will be pushed up. But the key thing for Forex is the fact that currencies are traded in pairs, and so you also have to consider one interest rate against the other. So fundamental analysis will, in part, involve knowing global interest rates, or at least the interest rates of the majors.

Inflation

Inflation is another key factor. A high inflation rate means that inside the country, the currency is losing value. High inflation rates may make investing in the currency of a given country a bad proposition. Once again, when looking at a given currency pair, you are going to want to make relative comparisons for the inflation rates in the two countries.

- GDP Growth Rates

When the GDP growth rate for a company is strong, this is going to attract more investment, generally speaking. Of course, there are many factors involved. If inflation is out of control, then high GDP growth rates may not be that attractive. But if all other indicators are good, a solid GDP growth rate is going to bring people to the table, which means that demand for the currency will be high.

Unemployment

The unemployment rate is another indicator of the health of the economy. High unemployment rates will make the currency unattractive, while lower unemployment rates are going to make the currency more attractive. Again, this is something that has to be seen in a relative context; you are going to compare the unemployment rate to the other partner in the currency pair. You will also want to look at the labor force participation rate if this data is available, as well as the number of people working full-time or part-time.

Trade

Trade issues can be important, too. When there is a lot of trade, there is also a lot of exchange of currency. For example, consider Japan, dollars flowing into the country need to be exchanged for Japanese Yen so that Japanese companies can use their profits at home. Besides trade, you will also want to look at any monetary flows between countries by large corporations, which eventually can mean having to exchange the currency into the local variety.

Indicators Of Forex Trading

Before we begin an in-depth discussion of the strategies used by Forex traders, you need to have an understanding of charts. The charts used in Forex are similar in a superficial sense to the charts that you may have seen on the stock markets. Typically, Forex traders are going to be using candlestick charts. In fact, this is almost a universal practice. That is the topic that we are going to cover in this chapter.

Remember What the Chart Is Charting

This sounds like a crazy statement, but you have to remember that the currency pair A/B means that if the value shown in the chart increases, this favors the currency A. What this means is that the value of currency A is increasing relative to the value of currency B. You can also look at it in the sense that if the graph on the chart is increasing, the value of currency B is decreasing.

So if you buy the currency pair A/B, and the increasing graph or upward trend is a trend that is working in your favor.

Now consider a downward trend. When the trend is going downward, you are losing money if you had bought the currency pair A/B, because this means that the value of currency A is decreasing relative to currency B.

Where some new traders get confused is when you sell the currency pair A/B. In this case, the meanings on the chart are reversed, because if you sell the currency pair A/B, this means that you are betting on the currency B. So when the chart is un an upward trend, if you had sold the currency pair you are losing money. This is easy to understand. For the sake of simplicity, let's say that you had sold the currency pair for $1. To exit the position, you have to buy back the currency pair. But if it increases in price to $2, then you would lose $1 buying it back. The values given here are for illustration only, but it nicely illustrates the general concept.

Now consider the opposite situation. That is, we are still talking about selling the currency pair A/B, but this time we see a downward trend on the chart. This means that the price of the currency pair is decreasing. We can, of course, frame this result in many ways. One of the ways that we can do so is to say that the currency B is increasing in value, with respect to currency A. Now let's say that once again we sold the currency pair A/B for $1. Now we imagine that is has decreased in price to $0.50. Then we can buy it back, and we make a $0.50 profit.

Of course, these prices are not realistic for a Forex trade, but it clearly shows the concept of how this actually works. If you understand the concept explained here, and you've understood how to read the change in pips from the chart and how to convert that into dollars moved based on your position size, then you are well on your way to becoming a Forex trader who at least understands what is going on.

What Is a candlestick

The next thing to come across is the use of candlesticks, which you always see on Forex charts. A candlestick is a graphical way to represent price action. By price action, we simply mean how high did the price go, how low did it drop, and what the opening and closing prices were. The candlestick charts also give a visual representation that we can eyeball, in order to see at a glance whether the price went up or down for a given time period.

So what each candlestick represents is a "trading session." The trading session can be one of many different lengths of time. Different traders are going to choose different lengths of time used for the trading sessions shown on the chart, depending on what their needs are. Some traders are interested in very short time frames, so they may use one-minute trading sessions. Others are going to use 5- or 15-minute trading sessions. You can also use 4-hour trading sessions or even one-day trading sessions. It's up to you to decide what time interval to use, and this is going to be decided in part by your trading style.

Before we show the basics of a candlestick, you need to understand how and why these are used. The basic idea that is behind the candlestick is to have a visual way to look at the chart and determine whether or not there is going to be a price reversal. Price reversals and trends are the bread and butter of this business. The first thing you are going to want to look for when you are trading currencies is if there is a trend one way or the other.

If there is a strong upward trend and there are signals that the trend is going to continue, then this is a currency pair that you want to buy. Conversely, if there is a downward trend, this could be a currency pair that you want to sell. This little fact that we have described is one important way that Forex trading differs from stock market trading, at least for most people. Granted, there are many people who trade options or who short stock, and they will make more complicated market plays. But you see with Forex that it automatically offers you ways to make money, no matter which way the market is moving. It's always in pairs, and you don't have to be wedded to one single currency.

That means that you don't have to be focused only on the dollar and hoping that it's going to always rise with respect to the Euro. As a Forex trader, you really should not care which direction the currency is moving. You can earn profits either way. The only time you care about which direction it's moving is after you've entered a position. Then and only then is the time that you need to be concerned about this issue.

Trend reversals are really the important thing to look for. If the market has been in a downward trend for some time, and you have been sitting on the sidelines, you are going to be looking for a trend reversal. It's never a good idea to get involved in a trade when it's too late. If you have been following the currency pair A/B and the currency pair has been in a long time downtrend, even if you like the currency B, you are probably better off waiting for a reversal, and buying the currency pair, rather than joining the trend late in the game. So in this example, when the candlesticks gave you the signal that the trend was reversing, you would buy the currency pair. The trend reversal signal would indicate that the downward trend has come to an end, and now is the time to get in a position in order to take advantage of the coming upward trend.

Structure Of A Candlestick

The candlestick has three parts. The first part is the rectangular area that is found in the center of the candlestick. This is called the body. The body of the candlestick tells you the opening and closing prices of the trading session. However, there are two types of candlesticks. Traditionally they are black and white, but I am going to skip over that because who uses black and white charts anymore. I can assure you that almost nobody does.

The background of most charts these days is either black or white. We are going to take the latter possibility, first because most Forex traders actually use black background charts. But you can use white backgrounds and some traders too.

There are two types of candlesticks. A candlestick can indicate that the price dropped for the trading period, in which case it is called a "bearish" candlestick. Or the candlestick can indicate that the price increased over the trading period, in which case it's a bullish candlestick.

On a chart with a white background, a bearish candlestick is red in color. A bullish candlestick will be green in color. On a black chart, the bearish candlesticks are usually solid white, and the bullish candlesticks are the green outline.

That is all pretty basic to understand. Now let us use a basic fact to explain the price action described or illustrated by a candlestick. If there is a bearish trading session, that means that the opening price was higher than the closing price. As a result, the top of the candlestick body – which is a higher pricing point – represents the opening price for the trading session. In contrast, the bottom of the candlestick, which is the lower price on the chart, represents the closing price for the trading session.

A bullish candlestick works in the opposite way. A bullish candlestick indicates that the price went up during the trading session. So the top of the candlestick is the closing price for the trading session. The bottom of the candlestick is going to be the opening price for the trading session.

A candlestick has lines that come out of the top and bottom of the body. These lines are called shadows or wicks. They have the same meaning whether or not the candlestick is bullish, or whether it's bearish. The wick or shadow coming out of the top of the candlestick body tells you the high price of the trading session.

The bottom wick tells you the low price of the trading session. The basics of candlestick setup are shown below.

Reversal Signals

Now we need to be able to look for certain signals that indicate a coming change in price trend. The signals are in the price action that tells us that traders are adopting a different sentiment, and the price is about to change direction. This is something you can spend a great deal of time educating yourself about. However, there is only a small subset of indicators that you need to be aware of.

Drawing Trend lines

Drawing trend lines is a simple method that can be used to determine where pricing is going to end up, if the market appears to be moving strongly in one direction or the other. No matter which direction the price is moving, there are always going to be fluctuations. So let's consider a downward trend first. A part of the fluctuation is the fact that on the way down, there are always going to be peaks that occur, that is the asset will drop in price, then rise back up for a short time, then drop in price again, and repeat the process, with each peak as it rises up again getting smaller and smaller. This natural feature of declining prices makes it easy to estimate trends. Starting at the top peak, draw a straight line from the top of the peak, passing the line through all the peaks on the way downward. You want to extend the line past the current price so that you can get an estimate of future price levels, if the market continues to decline. This will be a downward sloping line.

If you are looking at an upward trend instead, you start at the first dip or trough in price. Then draw a straight line, with an upward slope, that connects the bottoms of all the dips on the way up to the right of the chart. This will allow you to get an estimate of where the price is heading if the trend continues.

Most trading platforms allow you to draw trend lines right on their charts on the screen, so you don't actually have to print out a chart and do this on a piece of paper, to estimate where the price is going. You will simply have to position the line in the right locations.

Simple Moving Averages

One of the most popular of the other types of moving averages is called an exponential moving average. This moving average tends to give more accurate information. The reason that it's able to do so is that the exponential moving average weights the prices. The mathematical details aren't important for traders to know, you only have to note that when you use an exponential moving average, prices that are closer to the current trading period are given higher weights than long ago prices. This means that an exponential moving average curve is going to emphasize recent prices, as opposed to long ago prices.

The use of moving averages is so common that trading platforms, like metatrader, are going to show them below your pricing chart by default. An example is shown below, with crossover points indicated by the white arrows.

The way to do your analysis is to combine what you see with the candlesticks with what the moving averages are telling you. In my experience, the moving averages tend to be very accurate indicators of upcoming trends. However, it remains to be seen if the trend reversal is strong or long-lasting.

You can use a two-step process. The first step is to closely follow the candlestick patterns to look for indicators that a reversal is coming. If you see that the candlesticks are showing signs of a trend reversal, then you can check the moving averages to confirm or deny. If they confirm what you see on the candlestick charts, then you can make a move on a position, whether it is opening a new position or closing an existing position. So you can eyeball them with the candlesticks in real-time.

It can be good to practice with this before actually entering trades and putting real money at risk. Just spend a few days closely watching a currency pair, and begin to identify the patterns seen in the candlesticks in real-time.

Another chart option that you can look at is called the relative strength index or RSI. This can be used in conjunction with your other tools. The purpose of this indicator is to tell you if there are "overbought" or "oversold" conditions. Overbought means that there has been too much buying and that the price is higher than it should be. When there are overbought conditions, chances are there is going to be a trend reversal.

Oversold is the opposite situation; there has been too much selling off of the asset. In the case of oversold conditions, too many people sold the asset off, and as a result, prices have gone down to levels that are lower than conditions really justify.

The value of the RSI will tell you if conditions are neutral, overbought, or oversold. If conditions are neutral, the RSI will be ranging between 20 and 80. If conditions are overbought, this is demonstrated by an RSI that is higher than 80. Finally, if conditions are oversold, this is demonstrated by an RSI that is lower than 20. These values are not fixed, however. Some traders who are more conservative use a narrower range, such as 30-70.

Just like other indicators, you should not use the RSI in isolation, or take action based solely on what the RSI is telling you. Let's take the case of a rising price trend. If the RSI is telling you that the asset is overbought, you see a crossing of the short-term moving average below the long-term moving average, and the candlesticks are indicating a trend reversal, this is a strong selling signal.

Now consider in a downtrend. If the RSI falls below 20 indicating that the asset is oversold, and you see the short-term moving average crossing above the long-term moving average, with signals of a trend reversal coming from the candlesticks, then you have evidence that is strong enough to take as a buying signal. So you can see that we will take multiple signals together, to confirm what we see in the candlesticks. If the candlestick patterns are not confirmed, then you might want to hold off on making a buying decision.

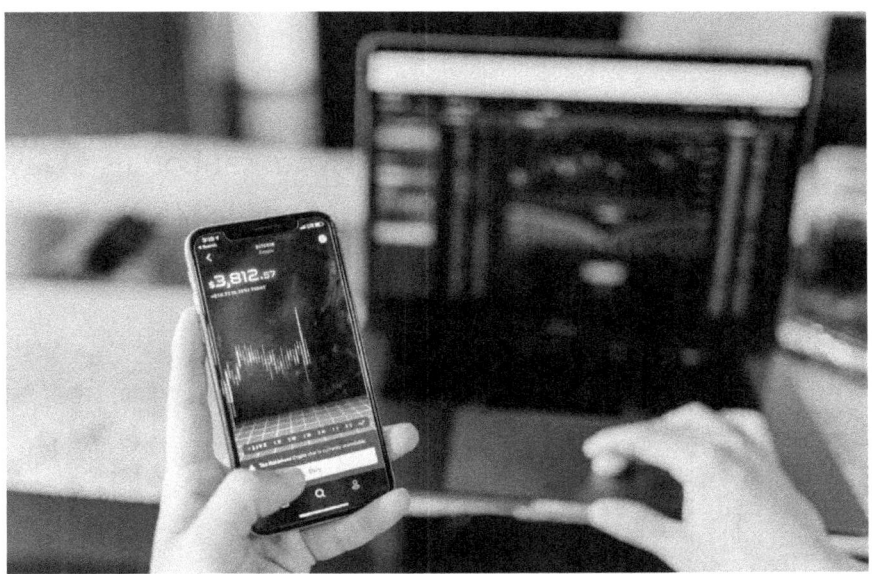

Chapter 3   Forex Trading Strategies

There are several types of forex strategies; however, it is important to choose the right one based preferred trading style to trade successfully. Some strategies work on short-term trades as well as long-term trades. The type of Forex strategies you choose depends on a few factors like:

• Entry points - traders need to determine the appropriate time to enter the market

• Exit point-trader need to develop rules on when to exit the market as well as how to get out of a losing position

• Time availability

If you have a full-time job, then you cannot use day trading or scalping styles

• Personal choices

People who prefer lower winning rates but larger gains should go for position trading while those who prefer higher winning rate but smaller gains can choose the swing trading

Common Forex Trading strategies include:

1. Range trading strategy

Range trading is one of the many viable trading strategies. This strategy is where a trader identifies the support and resistance levels and buys at the support level and sells at the resistance level. This strategy works when there is a lack of market direction or the absence of a trend. Range trading strategies can be broken down into three steps:

- Finding the Range

Finding the range uses the support and resistance zones. The support zone is the buying price of the security while the resistance zone price is the selling price of a security. A breakout happens in the event that the price goes beyond the trading range, whereas a breakdown occurs in the event that the price goes below the trading range.

- Time Your Entry

Traders use a variety of indicators like price action and volume to enter and exit the trading range. They can also use oscillators like CCI, RSI, and stochastics to time their entry. The oscillators track prices using mathematical calculations. Then the traders wait for the prices to reach the support or resistance zones. They often strike when the momentum turns price in the opposing direction.

- Managing Risk

The last step is risk management. When the level of support or resistance breaks, traders will want to exit any range-based positions. They can either use a stop loss above the previous high or invert the process with a stop below the current low.

Pros

- There are ranges that can last even for years producing multiple winning trades.

Cons

- Long-lasting ranges are not easy to come by, and when they do, every range trader wants to use it.
- Not all ranges are worth trading

2. Trend Trading Strategy

Another popular and common Forex Trading strategy is the trend trading strategy. This strategy attempts to make profits by analyzing trends. The process involves identifying an upward or downward trend in a currency price movement and choosing trade entry and exit points based on the currency price within the trend.

Trend traders use these four common indicators to evaluate trends; moving averages, relative strength index (RSI), On-Balance-Volume (OBV), and Moving Average Convergence Divergence (MACD). These indicators provide trend trade signals, warn of reversals, and simplify price information. A trader can combine several indicators to trade.

Pros
- Offers a better risk to reward
- Can be used across any markets

Cons
- Learning to trade on indicators can be challenging.

3. Pairs Trade

This is a neutral trading strategy, which allows pair traders to gain profits in any market conditions. This strategy uses two key strategies:

- Convergence trading - this strategy focuses on two historically correlated securities, where the trader buys one asset forward and sells a similar asset forward for a higher price anticipating that prices will become equal. Profits are made when the underperforming position gains value, and the outperforming position's price deflates

- Statistical trading - this is a short-term strategy that uses the mean reversion models involving broadly diversified Security Portfolios. This strategy uses data mining and statistical methods.

Pros

- If pair trades go as expected investors can make profits

Cons

- This strategy relies on a high statistical correlation between two securities, which can be a challenge.
- Pairs trade relies a lot on historical trends, which do not depict future trends accurately.

4. Price Action Trading

This Forex Trading strategy involves analyzing the historical prices of securities to come up with a trading strategy. Price action trading can be used in short, medium, and long periods. The most commonly used price action indicator is the price bar, which shows detailed information like high and low-price levels during a specific period. However, most traders use more than one strategy to recognize trading patterns, stop-losses, and entry, and exit levels. Technical analysis tools also help price action traders make decisions.

Pros
- No two traders will interpret certain price action the same way

Cons
- Past price history cannot predict future prices accurately

5.   Carry Trade Strategy

Carry trade strategy involves borrowing a low-interest currency to buy a currency that has a high rate; the goal is to make a profit with the interest rate difference. For example, one can buy currency pairs like the Japanese yen (low interest) and the Australian dollar (high interest) because the interest rate spreads are very high. Initially, carry trade was used as a one-way trade that moved upwards without reversals, but carry traders soon discovered that everything went downhill once the trade collapsed.

With the carry trade strategy:

1. You need to first identify which currencies offer high rates and which ones have low rates.
2. Then match two currencies with a high-interest differential
3. Check whether the pair has been in an upward tendency favoring the higher-interest rate currency

Pros
- The strategy works in a low volatility environment.
- Suitable for a long-term strategy
- Cons
- Currency rates can change anytime
- Ricky because they are highly leveraged
- Used by many traders therefore overcrowded

6. Momentum Trading

This strategy involves buying and selling assets according to the strength of recent price trends. The basis for this strategy is that an asset price that is moving strongly in a given direction will continue to move in the same direction until the trend loses strength. When assets reach a higher price, they tend to attract many investors and traders who push the market price even higher. This continues until large pools of sellers enter the market and force the asset price down. Momentum traders identify how strong trends are in a given direction. They open positions to take advantage of the expected price change and close positions when the prices go down.

There are two kinds of momentum:

- Relative momentum - different securities within the same class are compared against each other, and then traders and investors buy strong performing ones and sell the weak ones.
- Absolute momentum - an asset's price is compared against its previous performance.

Pros

- Traders can capitalize on volatile market trends
- Traders can gain high profit over a short period

- This strategy can take advantage of changes in stock prices caused by emotional investors.

Cons

- A momentum investor is always at a risk of timing a buy incorrectly.
- This strategy works best in a bull market; therefore, it is market sensitive
- This strategy is time-intensive; investors need to keep monitoring the market daily.
- Prices can shift in a different direction anytime

7. Pivot Points

This strategy determines resistance and support levels using the average of the previous trading sessions, which predict the next prices. They take the average of the high, low, and closing prices. A pivot point is a price level used to indicate market movements. Bullish sentiment occurs when one trades above the pivot point while bearish sentiment occurs when one trades below the pivot point.

Pros

- Traders can use the levels to plan out their trading in advance because prices remain the same throughout the day
- Works well with other strategies

Cons

- Some traders do not find pivot points useful
- There is no guarantee that price will stop or reverse at the levels created on the chart

8. Fundamental Analysis

This strategy involves analyzing the economic, social, and political forces that may affect the supply and demand of an asset. Usually, people use supply and demand to gauge which direction the price is headed to. The Fundamental analysis strategy then analyzes any factors that may affect supply and demand. By assessing these factors, traders can determine markets with a good economy and those with a bad one.

Forex Strategies for Beginners

When starting on Forex Trading, it important to keep things simple. As a beginner, avoid thinking about money too much and focus on one or two strategies at a time. The following three strategies are easy to understand and perfect for beginners.

1. Inside Bar Trading Strategy

This highly effective strategy is a two-bar price action strategy with an inside bar and a prior/mother bar. The inside bar is usually smaller and within the high and low range of the prior bar. There are many variations of the inside bar, but what remains constant is that the prior bar always fully engulfs the inside bar. Although very profitable, the inside bar setup does not occur often.

There are two main ways you can trade using inside bars:

- As a continuation move - This is the easiest way to trade inside bars. The inside bars are traded in trending markets following the direction of the trend.
- As a reversal pattern - the inside bars are traded counter-trend

When using this strategy, it is important to look for these characteristics when evaluating the pattern:

- Time frame matters - avoid any time frame less than the daily.
- Focus on the breakout - best inside bar trades happen after a break of consolidation where the preceding trend is set to resume.
- The trend Is your friend - trading with the trend is the only way to trade an inside bar

- A favorable risk to reward ratio is needed when trading an inside bar
- The size of the inside bar in comparison to the prior bar is extremely important

2. Pin Bar Trading Strategy

This strategy is highly recommended for beginners because it is easy to learn due to a better visual representation of price action on a chart. It is one of the easiest strategies to trade. Pin bars show a reversal in the market and, therefore, can be useful in predicting the direction of the price.

There are various ways traders trading with pin bars can enter the market:

- At the current market price
- Using an on-stop entry
- At limit entry, which is at the 50% retrace of the pin bar

To improve your odds when using the pin bar strategy:

- Trade with the trend
- Wait for a break of structure
- Trade from an area of value

Some of the mistakes pin bar traders should avoid include the following:

- Assuming the market will reverse because of a pin bar
- Focus too much on the pin bars and miss out on other trading opportunities
- All pin bars are not the same and should not be treated as such

3. Forex Breakout Strategy

A breakout strategy is where investors find stocks that have built strong support or resistance level, wait for a breakout, and enter the market when momentum is in their favor. This strategy is important because it can offer expansions in volatility, major price moves, and limited risk. A breakout occurs when the price moves beyond the support or resistance level. The breakout strategy is good for beginners because they can catch every trend in the market. Breakouts occur in all types of market environments.

Traders establish a bullish position when prices are set to close above a resistance level and a bearish position when prices close below a support level. Sometimes traders can be caught on a false breakout, and the only way to determine if it is a false breakout is to wait for confirmation. False breakout prices usually go beyond the support and resistance level; however, they return to a prior trading range by the end of the day.

Good investors plan how they will exit the markets before establishing a position. With breakouts, there are two exit plans:

- Where to exit with profit-traders can assess the stock recent behaviors to determine reasonable objectives. When traders meet their goals, they can exit the position. They can either raise a stop-loss to lock in profits or exit a portion of the position to let the rest run
- Where to exit with a loss - breakout trading show traders clearly when a trade has failed, and therefore they can determine where to set stop-loss order. Traders can use the old support or resistance level to close a losing trade

Pros

- You can catch every trend in the market

- Prices can quickly move in your favor

Cons

- Traders can get caught in a false breakout
- It can be difficult to enter a trade

Tips for trading breakouts:

- Never sell on breakdown or buy on breakout both carry extreme risks
- Trade with the trend
- Wait for higher volume to confirm a breakout
- Take advantage of volatility cycles
- Enter on the retest of support or resistance
- Have a predetermined exit plan

Note

Beginners are more likely to be successful in trade than their experienced counterparts are because they have not yet cultivated any bad habits. Experienced traders have to break bad habits and put aside any emotions built over the years.

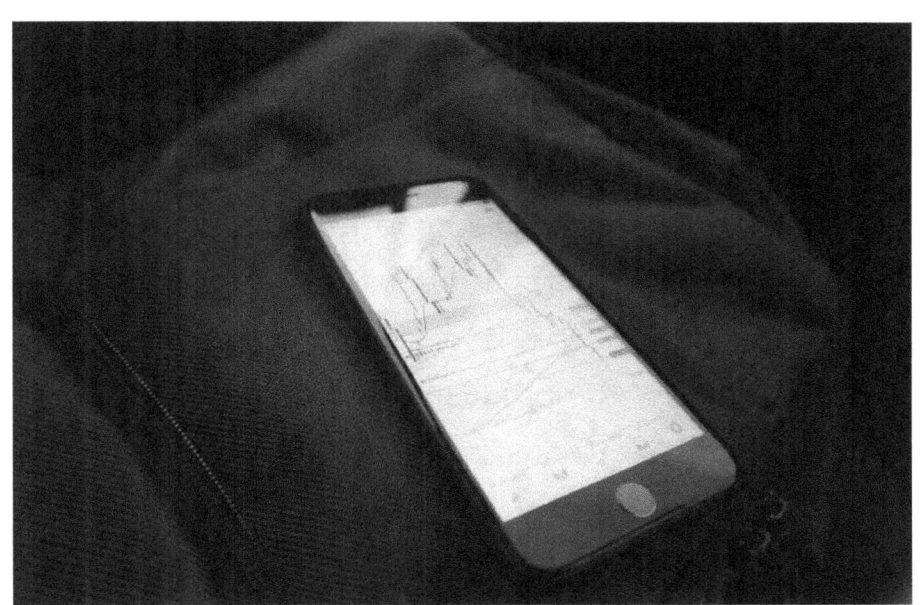

Chapter 4   Choosing A Broker

A broker refers to a firm or somewhat an individual who charges a certain fee or rather a commission for executing the buying and the selling process. In other words, they play the role of connecting the customer and the seller of the product. Thus, they are generally paid for acting as a link between the two parties. For instance, a client might be willing to buy shares from a particular organization. However, he might be lacking enough information about the places that he can purchase these shares. Thus, he will be forced to seek a person who understands well the stock exchange markets. The broker will, therefore, educate the client as well as link them with the right sellers. The broker will thus earn by offering such a connection. Other brokers sell insurance policies to individuals. In most cases, the individuals earn a commission once the clients they brought in the organization buy or renews the system. Any insurance companies have utilized the aspect as a way of increasing their sales.

List Of Common Brokers

IG   It is rated as one of the best forex brokers in the world. It was one of the pioneers in offering contracts for difference as well as spread beating. The organization was founded in the year 1974 and had been growing as a leader in online trading as well as the marketing industry. One of the aspects that have boosted its growth is the fact that it has linked a lot of customers, hence gaining more trust. In other words, a duet to its large customer base, a lot of clients prefers selling and buying their services. The other aspect worth noting is that this organization is London based, and it is among one of the companies that are listed on the London Stock Exchange market for more than 250 times. The aspect is due to the fact that it offers more than 15,000 products across several asset classes. Such classes include CFDs on shares, forex, commodities, bonds, crypto currencies as well as indices. Another aspect worth noting is that the 2019 May report, the firm is serving more than 120,000 active clients around the globe. Also, there are more than 350,000 clients that are served on a daily basis. The aspect has been critical in boosting its expansion as this group of individuals does more advertisements.

Some of the benefits that one gains by working in this industry are the fact that it allows comprehensive trading and the utilization of tools that enhance the real exchange of data. The other aspect worth noting is that it has a public traded license that allows a regular jurisdiction across the entire globe. In other words, one can acquire the services of this organization across the whole world with ease without the fear of acting against the laws of the nation. Also, the premises offer some of the competitive based commission that enhances pricing as spreading of forex. There is also a broad range of markets that are associated with the premises too, there several currencies and multi assets CFDs that are offered by the organization. The aspect has been critical in the sense that it allows the perfect utilization of all the services as well as the resources available across the globe. Some of the services that are offered by the organization are permitted globally, such that even after traveling from one nation to the other, one can still access their services. Since the year 1974, the organization has joined more than 195,000 traders across the entire globe. The aspect has allowed the selling its shares as well as services hence its fame.

Saxo Bank

The forex broker was established in 1992and has then been among the leading organization in offering forex services as well as the multi-asset brokerages across more than 15 nations. Some of these nations include the UK, Denmark, and Singapore, among others. One of the aspects of the organization is that it offers services to both retailers as well as institutional clients in the globe. The character has allowed the premises to provide more than one million transactions each day. Thus, it holds over $ 16 billion in asset management. The Saxo bank also offers more services to all of her clients. Such services include Spot FX, Non-deliverable Forwards (NDFs), contract difference as well as all the stock exchange options. The aspect has been critical in increasing its customer base across the globe. Some of the services such as crypto and bond services that are offered in the premises has allowed its expansion in the sense that they are sensitive and essentials.

Some of the benefits that one gain by assessing the services of the premises are that it enhances diverse selection of quality, it increases competitive commissions and forex spread as well as an improved multiple financial jurisdiction function that is allowed across the entire globe. In other words, the premises offer services that are allowed in the whole world, and that considers the rules and policies provided in each nation. The aspect has enhanced its continued growth despite the increased competition. One is required to pay a minimum deposit of about $2000 and an automated trading solution for all the traders. There are times when the premises offer bonuses of 182 trade forex pairs to all its clients. The aspect has also been the key reason behind its increased expansion. In other words, there are various services offered at a relatively low price hence the widening of its customer base.

CMC Markets

The premises were founded in 1989 and since then, it has grown to be one of the leading retail forex as well as a CFD brokerage. The premises thus serve more than 10,000 CFD instruments that cut across all the classes such as forex, commodities as well as security markets. The aspect has allowed the premises to spread its services to more than 60,000 clients across the entire globe. The premises have more than 15 offices that are well distributed in the nation; it offers the services. Most of its actions are thus related in UK, Australia as well as Canada. The aspect is due to the fact that the premises have it is customer bases in some of these nations. In other words, its serves are well are accepted in Canada and the UK.

There are various benefits that one gains by joining the premises. One, the premise offers some of the best competitive spread to all her customers. In other words, there are a variety of services that one can choose from. Also, the premises offer some of the largest selection of currency pairs in the entire industry. There are more than one hundred and eighty currencies that one can access by joining the premises. The other aspect worth noting is that the premises offer some of the best regulated financial agents in the entire globe. In other words, there are policies as well as rules that govern the provision of services in the world. Also, it is easy to identify the premises as there are potent charts as well as patterns that are used as recognition tools.

City Index

The forex broker was founded in 1983 in the UK. Since then, the premises have gained popularity and has turned out to be one of the leading brokers in London. It is worth noting that in 2015, the premises acquired GAIN Capital Holding Company that enhanced its increased customer base. Since 2015, the premises have been providing traders with services such as CFDs and spreading-betting derivatives. The premises have been further expanding the forex services with the acquisition of markets as well as FX solutions before gaining the capital market. Nowadays, the City Index has been operating as an independent brand under GAIN Capital in Asia as well as the UK. The aspect has allowed a multi-asset solution hence offering traders access to over 12,000 products across the global markets.

Some of the benefits that one gains part of the capital holding, a large selection of CFDs as well as regulated in several jurisdictions. The organization has tight spreads as well as low margins and fast execution. In others, the premises have been time from time, offering average ranges to all the clients; hence its increased customer base.

XTB Review

The organization was founded in Poland in the year 2002. Since then the organization has been well known for its forex and CFDs brokerage. Since then, the organization has maintained its offices in several nations; it offers its services. The premise has been working as a multi-asset broker that is regulated in several centers, hence increasing their competitive advantage. The premises have been trading as multiple financial centers offering a lot of services to all her traders. With a wide range of more than 2000 functions, the premises have been trading in almost all nations hence an increase in its customer base. The premises also offer excellent services that have been the reason behind its expansion. One of the aspects that have made the forex broker be thriving in such a competitive environment.

Signs Of Illegitimate Brokers

Although numerous brokers have been working in the forex industry, the aspect of legitimacy has been an issue affecting the progress of some these premises. One of the elements that are considered is the vulnerability of the clients. In most cases premises illegitimate brokers tend to rob of their customers. Most of them are self-reliant and optimistic. Most of them operate above their financial knowledge, hence making numerous mistakes. Most of these organization record big loses as they are relatively weak in term of management. The organization offers a lot of transactions that tend to be cumbersome in terms of management. It is worth noting that most of their operations aren't legitimate and never approved by the necessary authorities. Thus, when deciding on the kind of forex premises to seek services from, it is essential to consider some factors. Avoid assumptions that are exaggerative in terms of offering services that are above their knowledge. The aspect is harmful in the sense that they provide services that are not well planned hence recording a number of loses that befalls many clients in the long run. In other words, the drops recorded in the organization

Signs Of Legitimate Brokers

Although there are numerous illegitimate brokers in the market, there are legitimate brokers who offer excellent services. Most of them provide a few unique functions. In other words, they don't give a lot of transactions. Thus, they are able to manage their operations and command profits on their premises. The other aspect worth noting is that most of the services are approved by both the clients as well as the governing bodies in the organization. The other issue worth noting is that most of these premises have employed excellent knowledge in a range the progress of the customers. In other words, all their services are focused on advancing the clients.

In a nutshell, when selecting a forex broker, it is good to consider several factors. It is critical to find whether the premises are approved by both the governments as well as the clients. It is good to view the number of services as well as the transactions that are offered by the premise. The aspect is due to the fact that most of the wrong assumptions tend to provide numerous services that are poorly managed. The reviews offered by the clients of each of these premises need to be considered as they reflect whether the brokers are legitimate or not. Clients of consistent clients tend to offer reviews that are good as the services they receive manage to be excellent. The financial reports of these organization tend to be considered. The aspect is linked to the fact that they tend to reflect whether the brokers are making loses or profits. It is critical to find premises that record gains since the benefits tend to be high.

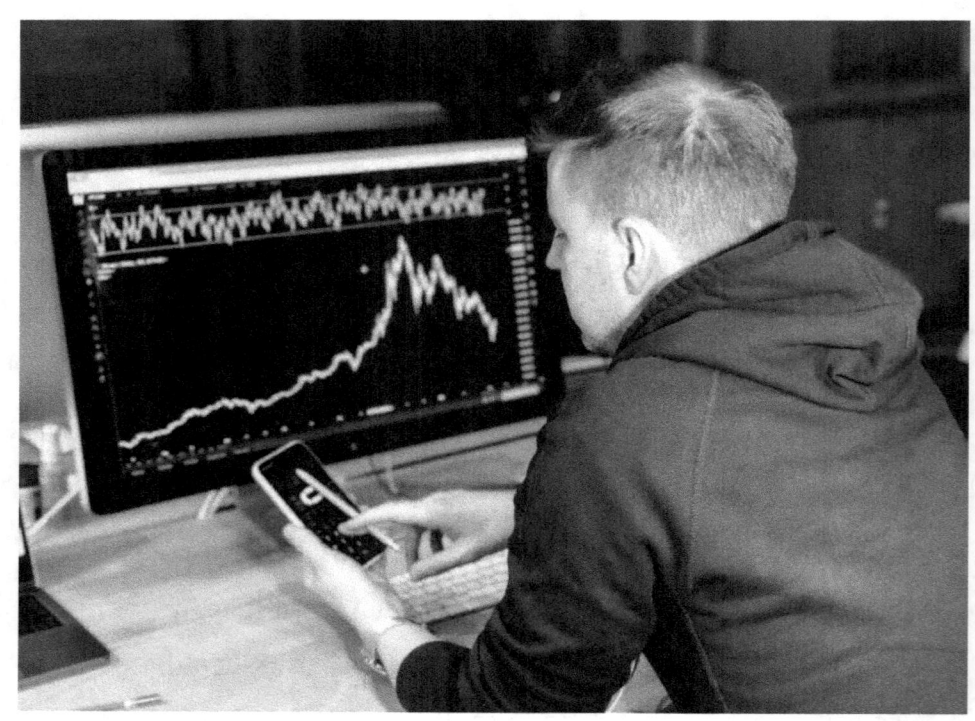

Chapter 5 Forex Market

Forex market is a market where you will buy, sell, exchange as well as speculate on the currencies. The market comprises of banks, retail forex brokers, hedge funds, central banks as well as investors. The currency market tends to be a financial market that has a tremendous amount of transaction, exceeding the combination of equity markets and futures. It is the most liquid of all the markets and the currencies traded against each other. Exchanging currencies is one of the most crucial things since that has to be there if people need to do foreign trade as well as business.

Despite being among the most significant market, there is no central place that the exchange takes place. All the transactions are done over-the-counter. The market is always open, and it is so in the entire world. You will find that the market is still active during day time and the price quotes change from time to time. The transactions will happen so that one can have a financial advantage. The fact that individual currency varies is what that will make the need for foreign exchange to raise.

When it comes to conducting trade, commercial as well as investment banks are in charge of doing that on their client's behalf. There are cases when individual and professional investors have the opportunity to trade in currency. But it is challenging for them, and it gives them a tough time. The internet has been a way that individual traders know more about the forex market.

For someone who is getting into the market for the first time, they will find it risky as well as complex to handle. There are different regulations, and there is standardization of the forex instruments. You can find cases where the market has no rules in some parts of the world. The banks that are in that trade will determine and be in a position to accept any risk that will come with the deal. They need to make sure that they are safe so that they will not suffer huge losses. That will be possible when they put an internal process in place. The bank will impose the regulations that it feels will work the best for them. The protection they require will be a determinant of the kind of riles that will put in place.

Any bank that is willing to participate in the forex market will provide an offer and a particulars currency bid. The way they will determine the prices will depend on the demand that there is in the market and the amount they and afford to supply. The traders cannot manage to influence any prices because the system has large trade flow. The method is vital in terms of creating transparency, and the investors can have access to the interbank dealing.

When you are a small retail trader, you are likely to have brokers who are not regulated and will re-quote the prices any time they wish. In some cases, they will even trade against you and take advantage of you. There may be some regulations, but that will depend on the area that your dealer is. The rules are not consistent in the whole world. So that you will know whether a dealer is under regulation or not, you need to take a thorough investigation. When you do that, you will get to know even where they are regulated. Seek to see the kind of protections that are there in case a crisis arises or the dealer's insolvency.

I a trader and you want to get in the trade and have no enough funds, day trading or swing trading is a comfortable option. If you have no issues with the limitation of funds, you can get in carrying trade or long-term fundamental-based trade. That will give you maximum profit, and you will find it worth investing your time and energy in the deal. For you to have high yields, you need to have a focus and understand the macroeconomic principles that drive the currency value. You need to have an experience with the technical analysis so that you will not be subject to losses. Know that the historical price will play a significant role in determining future rates. There is enormous data that is available out there in the market since it is done during the day and the night. That data will be useful for you to be in a position to determine the price movement in the future. For traders that like to use the technical tool, they will thrive in this market.

The prices in the forex market have a quotation of four decimal places since they have spread differences that are naturally very small. That makes it impossible to have a definitive rule on the number of decimal places that will be in forex quotes. You need to consider the risk that will come along with the trade before you get into the real currency trade. The trade-in currency is likely to be conducted in pairs. The pairs need to have low volatility as well as high liquidity. They are stable, add has well-managed economies having low chances of manipulation and smaller spread compared to other pairs. Some pairs consist of currencies from a small economy and those from a significant economy

Forex trading works in a way that the likelihood of making a profit is higher than that of making losses. Apart from benefit, numerous advantages will favor you when you get into a currency trade. The advantages of the forex market include and not limited to;

Flexibility

You are flexible when you get into the currency trade, and there are no restrictions and limitations of the capital that you will invest. The amount of money that has so that you can get into currency trade will not be a big issue. You can start small, and that will not hinder you from going to greater heights as time goes on. Some markets have a lot of rules that discourage people from getting in, and this is not the case in the currency market. The excess t=regulations are not present when it comes to the forex market.

The fact that it operates for twenty-four hours makes it a good idea since you can choose to trade at any given time. There are no restrictions, and you can even make the trade as a part-time job. Doing it as a full-time job is not a bad idea as such, and it will make you reap huge profits. The market is always open, and you do not have to wait for a specific time for it to open. You are free to hose the time that you want to do business which is different from other markets. In some markets, you have to wait for a particular session so that you will do trade. There are no situations likely to affect the forex market, and so you can trade at any time when you have the opportunity to do so. The market updates are available for you anytime you need to know how the market is doing. You will have a view of the trends that the trade is taking, and you will be in a position to decide wisely. You can trade at your convenience since there are numerous trading styles. For someone who wants to get in trade for a short time, the forex market is an excellent idea for them. You will have easy access to the forex market than any other market out there.

High Liquidity

There are vast numbers of people that are in foreign exchange in comparison to the ones in the financial market. It is highly liquid regardless of its size, and a lot of people get into the market every day. The big money orders that are out there will when the big players get into the market. There is only a small, or at times no price deviation at all even after the money gaps are filled by the big prayers. There being no price manipulation, efficient pricing is likely to be achieved, and there are no substantial deviations from the original price. Some people are ready to get into the business, and you can get someone to trade with any time you wish to purchase. Considering the levels of volatility, the price patterns remain constant. The market is efficient because of its high levels of liquidity, and the chances that competition will hit you hard are meager. Even with the large numbers of participants on every side, competition is not that severe. There is no likelihood of there being hitches, and transactions are always happening since the number of traders is relatively high. When you secure a position in the market, you stand a better chance since prices never change with a blink of an eye. That will help you to project the profits that you are likely to make when you make several transactions. The costs that are associated with the sales that you will make are not that high. The deals are done quickly, making it simple to have as many transactions as possible in a short period. You can predict the move that the prices are likely to take from time to time.

Highly Volatile

In the forex market, you can change from one currency to the other without much that from you. When you feel that specific money is having a considerable level of profit, you can shift to that so quickly. Since the aim to get into the trade is to make enough profit, that will be a good thing to do. When you know that a particular currency is likely to lower the price, you can leave that and go to the one that is a bit promising. Money-driven markets are likely to experience substantial losses. Due to the volatility level, some benefits come along with changing to a different currency which will give you good profits. Speculating on price changes from time and again will help you to stand in a safe position. Forex trading is satisfying when you compare to any other market. That is an added advantage and a sign to show you that your investment is safe in one way or the other. Short duration is there between opening and closing positions, and that means that significant opportunities to attract good profits are on the road.

Limited Entry Barriers

For you to invest in forex trade, you do not require a considerable amount of money as opposed to the requirements of other markets. Just a small initial capital is all you need to start trading currencies. There are no high amounts of deposits that you need to make for you to have an account. That is a unique advantage since some other markets need vast amounts of capital for you to start operating. It is cheap, making it simple for anyone willing to trade have the freedom to do so. If you are an average person, you will not find it hard to venture in the forex market. The market will attract people of all kind regardless of the amount of experience you have and the exposure. You do not have to worry that you will probably have many risks to deal with since there are low risks that come with forex trading. You need to organize and improve the skills you pose, and it will be a future benefit. Maturing the skills you have will not cost you much, and so that should not be the reason you why you do not want to invest in the forex market.

Great Tools to Help You Trade are at Your Disposal

When you get in the forex market, you will have great choices on the approaches that you will put in use to make sure that things will run smoothly. You can as well consider involving a specialist who will help you elevate your trading levels. They will equip you with fantastic knowledge on how to go about the forex market. When you have a full understanding of any market, you are likely to find it simple to find your way out. Different trademarks are there designed purposely for you to upgrade your trade and also consolidate news feeds. There are limits that you do not need to reach, and knowing them will help you manage risk in the right way. When you are financially unstable, there is a demo account that serves as an excellent resource. With time, you will establish whether it will be of any importance for you to own your account. Sharpening the trading that you pose from time to time will help you go a long way in the forex market.

There is Transparency

The transparency levels that are there on any information that you will access will draw you closer to the forex market. You have the freedom to access the rates any time you need to. It is made sure that the public access to such information, making you have confidence in the market. When you require any information, you do not have to wait for eternity even though the market size is big. The transparency in the entire thing will create goodwill, making you invest all that you have. You have your total control over any transaction that you want to make, and no one is there to follow you. If you do not agree with a specific transaction, you do not have to do that, and you have the free will. It is you to decide whether you want to trade with an individual trader or not. No one is in charge of accessing to what extent you are willing to risk and make a profit. That will solely depend on you and the zeal that you have to make money.

In case you are trading on behalf of an organization, make sure you do not invest your emotions as well. Take care of yourself, since the organization may find someone to replace you, making it unworthy the emotional investment you made. When things do not go the way, you desire them to go, take your time, and find out what went wrong when in the forex market. You will not invest your emotions, and you will have a successful trade. When a gap comes up, do not deal with it by hurting yourself. It will do more harm than ethical making you to hate forex trade which is an excellent experience to have.

Even though there are transaction costs that you will incur in the natural market conditions, they are of a considerate amount. Since there are no brokers in the middle, you are not going to deductions of commission when you realize a profit. That will mean that just a few expenses come along with forex trading. The fee you need to pay to a forex broker is relatively small when you compare to other securities. No clearing fees or any government deductions that you need to put into consideration. That means that the positive difference that you will make when you trade currencies will purely be profit.

Chapter 6   Forex Trading Psychology

Psychology and trading, most people might think that these factors don't relate to one another. Well, it very well does. As I mentioned earlier, most trading mistakes occur because the traders don't understand the importance of trading psychology. However, most traders don't trade successfully, mainly because of emotional problems. Especially, naïve traders don't handle emotions well, so they don't remain in the market for long. But, it is not something good which is why educating naïve traders is important. Even before they enter the market, it is important to spend the time to learn the market. However, the most common issue with trading is fear. But, fear is commonly seen when the trader moves into the live trading account. But, initially, the temptation is often found in naïve traders. When they enter the market, they enter with the thought of trading as much as possible to make money. Hence, this thought will not let them achieve what they actually should achieve. Therefore, when a trader is tempted to trade, he or she may trade even without analyzing or anticipating the trades.

However, as mentioned fear can also create a lot of issues in a trader's journey. Many traders give up trading completely because of fear. But, the fight or flight reaction is a human thing, that is commonly seen in traders. But actually, this reaction cannot be changed that easily, but of course, traders can handle this reaction wisely. If you study trading psychology, things will become simpler when trading the Forex market. Anyway, when you fear to trade, it will impact your trading behaviors negatively. Most of the time, you will look for a safer method to trade and, perhaps, it is not possible to find safer trading methods in the Forex market.

As you already know, the Forex market involves a lot of risks, so as traders, you must learn to handle them carefully. For example, when you enter into a trade, your instincts point out the chances of losing and you will eventually exit from the trade, and it might have been a profitable trade. So see, your mind has a direct connection to the way you trade.

Even if you have a defined plan, you can still steer away from trading because the power of psychology is immense. You might even become anxious and consider short-term positions because you are afraid to enter into long-term positions even if they seem profitable. Well, yes, fear, greed, and all the other emotions can cause a lot of problems to your trading journey. Hence, you must understand trading psychology. If you do, you will be able to assist those emotions wisely and handle trading successfully. Normally, if you overcome fear, it will be beneficial to your trading journey as well as life.

Typically, traders don't fear the market when they are preparing to enter into a trade, but when the market opens, their emotions play the role. As humans, you can never get rid of emotions because it is a part of humankind. But, you can always learn the methods to control your emotions when excitement is a dangerous emotion when trading the Forex market. When you are excited, you might make mistakes when entering a trade or anticipating market movements. Thus, when you are trading, you have to try to keep your emotions neutral.

Most traders succumb to accept that they are making trading mistakes that are related to psychology. But normally, when people can't accept, denial is the first reaction. Over time, they tend to accept the truth. Just like that, even the naïve traders will learn to accept the truth. However, Forex trading is not only about trading system and strategies. You must accept that mindset is an important part of Forex trading. The way you anticipate the Forex market has a lot to do with trading. Also, only if you understand the trades will you be able to enter into it. Thus, a trader's mindset has a lot to do with trading.

If you look at certain websites that advertise robotic trading systems, you might find trading psychology as an absurd thing. But, remember, those trading systems will not provide benefits as they portray. Nothing is as best as trading manually. You must use your knowledge and skills to trade the market; only then will you be able to trade successfully. Also, those websites are doing their duty to market their product, and if you rely on them and purchase it, you might have to pay them for using their product. Hence, when you come across something like this, make sure to think logically. As a beginner, you must try to settle for a simple yet effective strategy, so that you will be able to trade peacefully.

Anyway, why do you think most naïve traders struggle to make money? You might have seen many people who fail in trading the Forex market. Well, there are many reasons why traders fail, but the major reason is the ones who enter the Forex market don't really know the market. A higher percentage of traders enter into the Forex market by believing the fabricated ads. And it makes them set unrealistic goals. Eventually, they struggle to meet those unrealistic goals and end up quitting trading. But the worst part is that there are traders who quit their day job after they enter the Forex market. Well, it is not a wise move because they must test to check whether trading works for them. Or some other traders believe trading is easy money and no matter how many times I repeat it, some people still believe it is possible. These thoughts create tension and stress, so eventually, the trader becomes emotionally unstable. Thus, when traders trade with an emotionally unstable mindset, they lose money.

Psychology Of A Successful Trader In The Forex Market

So, how can a trader develop a trading mindset? If you want to develop a trading mindset, you need to do your part. It is important to put the required effort to accomplish what you are looking for. Well, you can't build a trading mindset that quickly because you have to learn and accept the Forex market as it is. If you try to deny facts about the Forex market, you will not be able to create a trading mindset.

You must start developing your trading mindset by handling the risks in trading. First of all, understand that risk management isn't for one trade, preferably it is applicable for all the trades that you enter into. You must make sure to calculate the risk for each trade before you enter into it. When you are managing risks, certain emotions might try to confuse you, but you must not let it happen. Once you start handling your emotions wisely, you will be able to manage trades also. However, the simplest way to control emotion when managing risks is to risk ONLY the amount that you can lose. You must create a mindset that enters into a trade while knowing the probability of losing trade. If you follow this, you will be able to remain in the trading world for a long time. But, it takes practice and patience to create a trading mindset that accepts losses. Also, you must master your trading edge. No matter what trading strategy you are using, you must know it completely to trade successfully.

And, remember, overtrading will never create profits. Instead, overtrading will blow all your hard-earned money. You must trade only when you actually see a profit signal. Don't try to trade just because you feel like trading. Or don't try to guess trade because that doesn't work in Forex trading. If you overtrade, it can be challenging to stop, and you'll become an emotional trader.

If you want to build a trading mindset, you must have an organized mindset. So, basically, when you have an organized mindset, you will think about the trading plan, journal, and much more. You must accept the fact that Forex trading is a business. Hence, don't try to gamble in the market. When you are making trading decisions, you must remain calm and steady; only then will you be able to think clearly.

But then, after you build a trading mindset, you must not let emotions play their role. However, the most common emotions that you must avoid are:

Euphoria

You might argue that euphoria is good, yes, it is good. But when it is related to the Forex market, it becomes dangerous. For example, if a trader wins a few profitable traders, he or she might become confident when trading the next trade. Well, it is good to feel confident when entering the next trade, but feeling overly confident is not a good thing. When traders become overly confident, they don't watch or study the market as they did before. The consecutive profitable trades should not get into your mind and increase the level of confidence. When trading Forex if you are overconfident, you will not be able to accept the loss if the trade doesn't react the way you wanted. Hence, it is better to remain calm even if you make profits continuously.

Fear

Most traders who enter the market with no knowledge about trading tend to fear the market. Also, some traders might fear because they cannot effectively trade using any specific strategy. However, usually, when a trader continuously experiences losses, he or she may tend to fear to trade. Perhaps, it is understandable because losing hard-earned money isn't easy. But, you can avoid the mistake of risking more than the amount that you are comfortable with. Most naïve traders don't follow this rule even if we keep repeating it. If fear persists, you will not be able to trade better trades or become successful. It has the power to keep you away from good trades as well. Hence, try to overcome fear by limiting the amount you risk in trading. For the naïve traders, start your journey on a demo account without directly entering the live account. If you do so, you'll be able to learn to control emotions.

Greed

You might have heard that people say only bulls and bears make money, but pigs get slaughtered. If you don't understand what it means, it means greed. If you are greedy, you will not be able to make money in the market. Instead, you will be kicked out of the market. Mostly, traders become greedy when they don't have self-discipline. Most traders make quick decisions when the market shows profitable trade signals, but it is not recommended. Instead, you must be calm and collected. Take some time to understand the market, focus on the risk ratio, set a plan, and then enter into the trade. Also, remember, if you are risking more than what you are ready to lose, it apparently shows your level of greed to make money. Thus, you must overcome greed if you don't want to lose your account.

Revenge

This is one of the funny behaviors of traders because what is the point in revenging the market? For the Forex market, you are just one amongst the millions, and it doesn't make sense. However, if you are trying to revenge trade just because you lost a few trades, remember, this might lead to further losses. When you are emotional, you will not be able to make wise decisions. Hence, you must wait for some time until your mind is stable and ready to trade.

So, when learning the psychology of trading, you might find it exciting. But, success can decide when you take these things into practice. You don't have to try these tips and ideas on the live account, instead use the demo account. The Forex market is one of the best markets because it has provided solutions for almost all the issues. So, as traders, if you solve your personal trading issues, you will be able to become a successful trader.

Mass Psychology And Its Measures

Following are a list of things required for becoming a successful Forex trader

Trading plan: A forex trader should have a trading plan that should be prepared well in advance. The trading plan should list out his entry and exit conditions as well as his money management rules. This is of utmost importance and he should religiously follow his trading plan to the tee. In order to become a successful forex trader, he should never deviate from the trading plan.

Discipline: This is one of the most important qualities needed to be a successful forex trader. A trader should be disciplined and methodical in the way he goes about with forex trading. He should not only meticulously plan his trading, but should also be disciplined enough to follow it.

Ability to do analysis: A forex trader should have the ability to analyze the technical charts and other financial data in order to become a successful forex trader. He should invest in himself and learn how to use the financial tools that would help in becoming a better trader. Trading is a very competitive job and one needs to be always one step ahead of others in order to be successful.

Emotional stability: It is very important to keep emotions and trading separate. In order to be successful, the trader should be able to trade like a machine and not let emotions affect his trades. He shouldn't let losses affect him nor should he get overly excited about the winning trades.

Hard work: Nothing beats hard work for becoming a successful forex trader. The trader should be prepared to put in a lot of hours and research the forex market thoroughly before each trading day. Most successful forex traders have a pre-trading session wherein they analyze the global markets, check charts, read various financial newspapers, note down key economic events of the day etc. before they start their trades.

Good knowledge of charting and analysis tools: In order to be a successful forex trader, it is very important to have good knowledge on the usage of charting and other analytic software. The usage of these trading software's raises the odds of success considerably, so it is important to have a good understanding of them.

Constant Learning: Trading field requires constant learning. The trader should be prepared to learn throughout his trading career. Something that might work now might not work after 5 years. So it's very important to constantly adapt and keep learning in order to be a step ahead of others. A good trader should be on the constant look out of learning new things that might help him with his trading be it the usage of a trading software or a new way of analysis.

Mastering fear: It is very important to master fear in order to be a successful forex trader. The trader should be prepared to take losses now and again and should understand that it's a part and parcel of the game. The inability to book losses and holding on to a losing position can result in more losses. The trader should also be ready to take a trade when a good opportunity arises and should not allow fear to hold him back.

Thinking on your own: It is very important to think on your own and make trading decisions and to not just blindly follow the crowd. As the saying goes, "buy into the fear and sell into the greed!" Now, this does not mean to always do the opposite to what others do. It just means that the trader should have an open mind and should have the ability to think on his own and make decisions accordingly.

Awareness of the global events: Forex markets are affected by the major international events that occur. So it's important to have an understanding of the key economic events happening globally as the forex markets are traded globally and affected by these economic events. A few examples of the key economic events are Federal Bank interest rate decision, ECB rate decision, GDP data of key economies, job data of key economies, inflation data of key economies etc.

Never blame the market: The market might behave irrationally but the trader should be responsible for reading the market cues and making trading decisions. Instead of playing the blame game he should learn from each mistake and learn from it. The trader should understand the risks associated with trading and have a proper money management rule in place.

Trading journal: It is important to maintain a trading journal and make an entry of all the trades he makes. The reasons for taking that particular trade should also be noted down. This would help in analyzing the trades later and help in avoiding the mistakes made. This would also help in identifying the good trades made and look for similar patterns later on.

Choosing the right broker: It is important to choose the right broker. Some of the factors that should be considered while selecting a broker should be a) low brokerage b) fast and reliable trading terminal c) ease of trading and good research and charting software's that the broker provides.

Money management rules: This is perhaps the most important among all things that are mentioned till now. A money management rule is basically the rules that define the maximum loss a trader can afford to take per trade or at a point of time. Most forex traders never risk more than 2- 5 % per trade. They also never risk more than 10-20 % at a particular point across all trades. It is very important to follow these rules; else you run the risk of wiping out your entire trading account in a matter of days, if not hours! It is always better to limit your losses and live to fight another day!

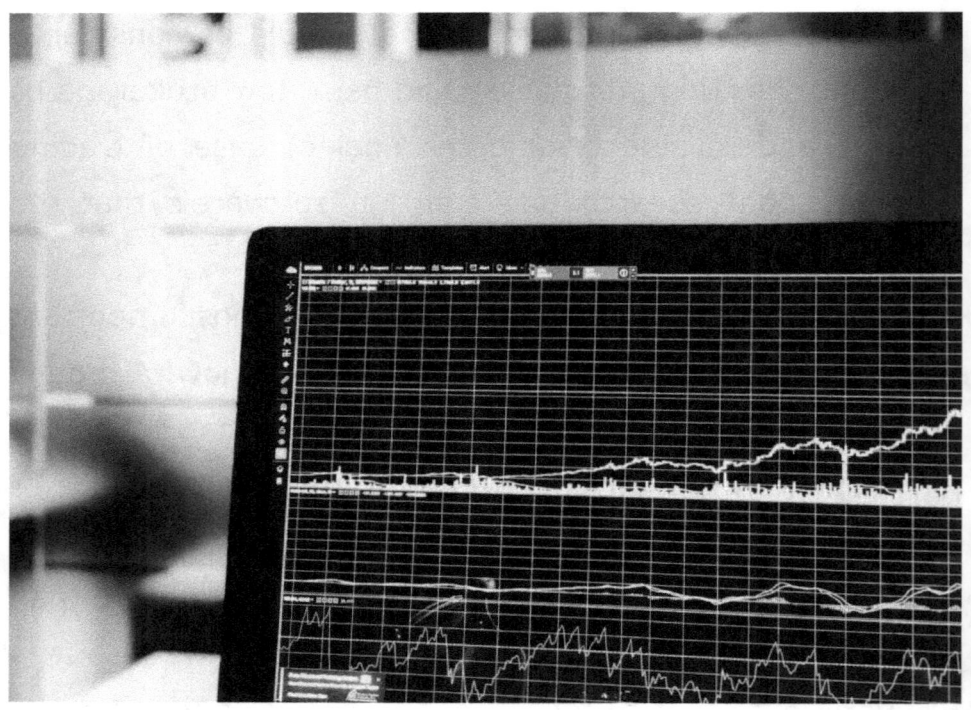

Chapter 7   Money Mistake to avoid

Now we'll turn our attention to giving some tips, tricks and advice on errors to avoid in order to ensure as much as possible that you have a successful time trading.

Avoid The Get Rich Quick Mentality

Any time that people get involved with trading or investing, the hope is always there that there's a possibility of the big winning trade. It does happen now and then. But quite frankly, it's a rare event. In many occasions, even experienced traders are guessing wrong and taking losses. It's important to approach Forex for what it really is. It's a business. It is not a gambling casino even though a lot of people treated that way so you need to come to your Forex business–and it is a business no matter if you do it part-time, or quit your job and devote your entire life to it–with the utmost seriousness. You wouldn't open a restaurant and recklessly buy 1 thousand pounds of lobster without seeing if customers were coming first. So, why would you approach Forex as if you were playing slots at the casino? Take it seriously and act as if it's a business because it really is. Again, it doesn't matter if you officially create a corporation to do your trades or not, it's still a business no matter what. That means you should approach things with care and avoid the get rich quick mentality. The fact is the get rich quick mentality never works anywhere. Unfortunately, I guess I could say I've been too strong in my assertion. It does work on rare occasions. It works well enough that it keeps the myth alive. But if we took 100 Forex traders who have to get rich quick mentality, my bet is within 90 days, 95% of them would be completely broke.

Trade Small

You should always trade small and set small achievable goals for your trading. The first benefit to trading small is that this approach will help you avoid a margin call. Second, it will also help you set profit goals that are small and achievable. That will help you stay in business longer.

Simply put, you will start gaining confidence and learning how to trade effectively if you get some trades that make $50 profits, rather than shooting for a couple of trades that would make thousands of dollars in one shot, but and up making you completely broke. Again, treat your trading like a real business. If you were opening a business, chances are you would start looking for slow and steady improvements and you certainly would not hope to get rich quick.

Let's get specific. Trading small means never trading standard lots. Even if you have enough cash to open an account such that you could trade standard lots, I highly recommend that you stay away from them. The large amount of capital involved and margin that would be used could just get you into a lot of financial trouble. For beginners, no matter how much money you are able to devote to your trading, I recommend that you start with micro lots. Take some time and learn how to trade with the small lots and start building your business earnings small profits at a time. Trading only with micro lots will help in force discipline and help you avoid getting into trouble. Make a commitment only to use micros for the first 60 days. After that, if you have been having decent success, consider trading a mini lot. You should be extremely cautious for the first 90 days in general.

Be Careful With Leverage

Obviously, it's extremely beneficial. It allows you to enter and trades that would otherwise not be possible. On the other hand, the temptation is there to use all your leverage in the hopes of making it big on one or two trades. You need to avoid using up all your leverage. Remember that you can have a margin call and get yourself into big trouble if your trades go bad. And it's important to remember there's a high probability that some of your trades are going to go bad no matter how carefully you do all your analysis.

Not Using A Demo Account

A big mistake the beginners make, is jumping in too quickly. There is a reason that most broker-dealers provide demos or simulated accounts. If you don't have a clue what that reason is, let's go ahead and stated here. Brokers provide demo accounts because Forex is a high-risk trading activity. It can definitely be something that provides a lot of rewards and it does for large numbers of traders. But there is a substantial risk of losing your capital. Many beginners are impatient hoping to make money right away. That's certainly understandable, but you don't want to fall into that trap. Take 30 days to practice with a demo account. This will provide several advantages. Trading on Forex is different than trading on the stock market. Using the demo account, you can become familiar with all the nuances of Forex trading. This includes everything from studying the charts, to placing your orders and, most importantly, understanding both pips and margin. The fact that there is so much leverage available means you need to learn how to use it responsibly. You need to know how to experience going through the process and reading the available margin and so forth on your trading platform while you are actually trying to execute trades. A demo account let you do this without risking real capital. It is true that it's not a perfect simulation. The biggest argument against demo accounts is that they don't incorporate the emotion that comes with trading and real money. As we all know, it's those emotions, including panic, fear and greed, that lead to bad decisions. However, in my opinion, that is a weak argument against using demo accounts. The proper way to approach it is to use a demo account for 30 days and then spend 60 to 90 days doing nothing but trading micro lots. Don't worry, as your micro trading lots you can increase the number of your trades and earn profits. While I know you're anxious to get started, keeping yourself from losing all your money is a good reason to practice for 30 days before doing it for real.

Failing To Check Multiple Indicators

There is also a temptation to get into trades quickly just on a gut level hunch. You need to avoid this approach at all costs. Some beginners will start learning about candlesticks and then when they first start trading, they will recognize a pattern on a chart. Then in the midst of the excitement, they will enter a large trade based on what they saw. And then they will end up on the losing end of a trade. Some people are even worse and they don't even look at the candlesticks. Instead, they just look at the trend and think they better get in on it and they got all anxious about doing so. That means first checking the candlesticks and then confirming at least with the moving average before entering or exiting a position. You should also have the RSI handy and you may or may not want to use Bollinger bands.

Use Stop Loss And Take Profit Orders

Well, I hate to repeat myself yet again, but this point is extremely important. I am emphasizing it over and over because it's one of the tools that you can use in order to protect yourself from heavy losses. One of the ways that you can get out of having to worry about margin calls and running out of money is to put stop-loss orders every time you trade. This will require studying the charts more carefully. You need to have a very clear idea where you want to get out of the trade, if it doesn't go in the direction you hoped. But if you have a stop-loss order in place, then you can avoid the problem of having your account just go down the toilet. Secondly, although the temptation is always there to look for as many profits as possible, in most cases, you should opt to set a take profit order when you make your trade. That way you set as we said, distinct boundaries which will ensure that you make some profit without taking too much risk. The problem with doing it manually is that excitement and greed will put you in a position where are you miss the boat entirely. What inevitably happens, is people get too excited hoping to earn more profits and they stay in the trade too long. The Forex market changes very fast and so what eventually happens is people that stay into long inevitably and up with a loss. Or at the very least they end up missing out on profits.

There is one exception to this point. There are some times when there is a distinct and relatively long-term upward trend. If you find yourself, by doing the analysis and determining that such an upward trend is here, that might be an exception to the rule. In that case you want to try to ride the trend and maximize your profits.

Remember Price Changes Are In Pips

Beginners often make the mistake of forgetting about pips. If you have trouble with pips and converting them to actual money, go back and review the examples we provided. Remember that pips play a central role in price changes, you need to know your dollar value per pip in order to keep tabs on your profit and losses. This is also important for knowing the right stop loss and take profit orders to execute.

Don't Try Too Many Strategies Or Trading Styles At Once

When you are a beginning Forex trader, it can be tempting to try everything under the sun. That can be too much for a lot of people. The most advisable thing to do is to stick with one strategy so don't try scalping and being a position trader at the same time. The shorter the time frame for your trades, the more time and energy, you have to put into each trade. Scalping and day trading are activities that would require full-time devotion. They are also high-pressure and that can help enhance emotions involved in the trades. For that reason, I don't really recommend those styles or strategies for beginners. In my opinion and to be honest it's mine alone, I think position trading is also too much for a beginner. It requires too much patience.

Perhaps the best strategy to use when you're beginning Forex trading is to become a swing trader. It's a nice middle ground, in between the most extremely active trading styles and something that is going to try people's patience such as position trading. When you do swing trading, you can do time periods longer than a day certainly, but as long or short as you need to meet your goals otherwise. Swing trading also takes off some of the pressure. And it gives you more time to think and react.

This does not mean that you can't become a scalper or day trader at some future date. What I am advising is that you gain some experience using more relaxed trading styles before taking that path. And believe me, swing trading is going to be challenging enough.

Market Expectations

Life as a forex trader can sometimes get lonely. After all, this is the kind of career where you are completely on your own. You enjoy your profits alone, but you also suffer losses on your own. There is no one in the forex market whom you can depend on to comfort you. Therefore, it is also good if you connect with like-minded people. Feel free to make friends with other traders. After all, you are all players in the market who want the same thing. The good thing is that you are not competing with one another. In fact, you can even help one another by sharing information, insights, and strategies. Thanks to the Internet, it is very easy to find and connect with people who are also interested in forex trading. You simply have to join an online group or forum on forex trading. You can do this quickly with just a few clicks of a mouse. You can then make a public post or even send a private message to any member of the group/forum. If you have a neighbor or friend who also likes trading currencies, then you can invite him out for a coffee one of these days. Connecting with like-minded people is not just a way to learn but it can also inspire you to become a better trader.

- Have fun

Forex trading is fun. This is a fact. In fact, many traders get to enjoy this kind of life that they still continue to learn it despite their losses. It is also not uncommon to find traders, especially beginners, who spend their whole day just learning about forex trading. Like gambling in a casino, trading currencies can also be very addicting, especially if you are making a nice profit from it.

Learn to have fun and enjoy the journey. Sometimes taking things too seriously can ruin the experience and even make you less effective. In your life as a trader, you will definitely make some mistakes from time to time. You will experience losing money from what otherwise would have been a profitable trade if only you knew better. Do not get too stressed. The important thing is for you to learn as much as you can from every mistake. Take it easy, but remember to learn from the experience. Making mistakes is part of the learning process. Of course, you should try to minimize them as much as possible. Learn and have fun.

Risk Management

Risks do occur in every sphere of life. However, when it comes to trading in forex securities, these risks, more so, financial risks are enhanced. This is due to the volatility of the foreign exchange currencies.

Nature of Forex risk

Forex risk (currency risk, FX risk or exchange rate risk) is a risk (financial) that prevails when a financial transaction is monetized in a foreign currency. When it comes to multinationals, forex risk occurs when one or several of its subsidiaries maintain financial records and statements in currencies other than those of the parent entity. When it comes to a multinational, there is a risk that there could be negative movements in foreign currency of the subsidiary entities in relation to the domestic currency of the parent entity prior to the report being compiled. International traders are also exposed to this risk.

Types of forex risks

There are many types of forex risks. Nonetheless, the following are the major types of forex risk:

Transaction risk – This occurs where a firm has cash commitments whose values are subject to unforeseeable changes in exchange rate due to a contract being considered in foreign currency. The cash commitments may include account receivables and account payables.

- Economic risk – A firm is exposed to economic risk when its market value is susceptible to unanticipated changes in forex rate. This may affect the firm's share value, present and future values of cash flows, firm's market position and ultimately firm's overall value.

- Translation risk – Translation risk affects mainly multinational firms. Thus, a firm's translation risk is the susceptibility of its financial statements and reports to forex changes. This happens when a parent firm has to prepare consolidated statements, including those of its foreign subsidiaries. This largely affects the firms reported income. This also affects its stock value in the securities market.

Contingent risk – Contingent risks occurs when a firm engages in foreign contracts thus resulting in foreign-denominated obligations. Such foreign contracts may include bidding for foreign projects, commitments to foreign direct investment (for example, investing in foreign subsidiaries), and settling legal disputes involving foreign entities.

Forex risk management

Several strategies exist to safeguard against forex risks. Some of these strategies include:

- Forex hedging strategies – This covers transaction exposure. Use of money market tools and derivatives can help reduce these risks. Futures contracts, options, forward contracts, and swaps are some of these derivatives. Some operational techniques to support these strategies include payments and exposure netting, leading and lagging of receipts, and currency invoicing.
- Translation exposure strategies - These are strategies aimed at risks that are primarily due to prevailing reporting standard (or differences in reporting standards between the parent company and its foreign subsidiaries), which mainly affect the net assets and net liabilities. This can be mitigated through hedging the balance sheet. In this regard, a firm can purchase a commensurate amount of exposed assets or liabilities to balance off any discrepancy due to forex rates. A business entity can also hedge against translation exposure by using Forex derivatives.
- Alternative strategies to manage economic or operating exposure can also be adopted.

This may involve carefully selecting production sites with a clear intent to cut down on production cost, flexible approach to sourcing of supplies on the international markets, diversification in the export market. Creating product differentiation through extensive research and development can also help in hedging against economic risks.

Forex risk management tools and techniques

Several tools and techniques that you can employ in the forex risk management. These tools and techniques include:

Forward Contract
- Limit Orders
- Stop Loss Orders

Options

Forward contract

A forward contract allows a user to hedge expected forex transactions by locking in a price today for a transaction that will take place in future. This enables the trader to eliminate or mitigate risks of exchange rate fluctuations. Forward contracts can last for as long as a year.

Limit Orders

154

You can use Limit Orders in transactions that do not have time-restricted payment obligations. Thus, a business can set an ideal exchange rate at which to buy a particular currency. For example, if the current exchange rate is EUR/0.72GBP, a businessperson may not wish to send £50,000 to the UK until he can get a better rate. He can make a limit order to his payment provider target a rate of EUR/0.75GBP. When this rate is attained, a transfer is triggered, and funds are automatically sent to the UK.

Stop Loss Orders

Stop loss orders guarantees a minimum rate at which a currency is exchanged by allowing a trader to lock in a deal so that it never trades below what he considers as an acceptable exchange rate. It is, in essence, an instruction to buy or sell a currency at a predetermined 'worst case' exchange rate.

Options

An option is a risk management tool in forex transactions. It protects businesses from downturns in the currency market, but also allows them to take advantage of positive currency shifts. When a business buys an option it secures the right, but not the obligation, to make an international purchase or exchange funds at a predetermined exchange rate on a chosen date. Where Options differ to FECs is that the buyer is not obligated to settle on that date. If movements in the forex market present more favorable exchange rates than the rate that was set when the Option was bought, the buyer is not obliged to settle.

Tips and hacks on risk management:

Set Orders – Limit orders, stop orders, trail orders, etc
- Set risk/reward ratio
- Set win-rate

Blend win-rate and risk/reward ratio to derive the most optimal strategy

Focus less on short-term performance targets and more on mid-term and long-term performance targets

Carry out position sizing
- Blend R-Multiple with Risk/Reward ratio to balance between performance and potential

Make spread vs. fees comparison for net profit
- Watch out for correlations – pairs that are positively correlated increase your risks

BACKTESTING

Backtesting is the process of testing your trading strategy on previous historical data to establish its efficacy and reliability in as far as establishing how accurately the strategy would have predicted the actual result. Thus, if the strategy works on historical data, then, it is expected to work on the current and future data.

Why carry out Backtesting?

The following are some of the important reasons as to why you need to carry out Backtesting:
- To test the efficacy and reliability of your trading strategy.
- To iron out flaws in your strategy so as to improve its efficacy and reliability.
- To cut down on risks that would arise due to unreliable strategy.
- To have an insight into how your intended forex system is going to work.

- To refine your trading strategy parameters.

Types of Backtesting

There are two main types of backtesting:

Manual backtesting.

- Automated backtesting.

Manual backtesting

In manual backtesting, you largely design your own testing system. You manually enter and exit the markets.

Advantages

- You can have the look and feel of your system as you enter and exit the market.
- You can easily customize the system to your unique needs.

Disadvantages

- Time consuming.
- Reliability is not guaranteed.

Automated backtesting

In automated backtesting, you create a system that automatically enters or exits the market on your behalf. You take advantage of the already existing backtesting systems in the market.

Advantages
- Less susceptible to your emotions
- Automate income generation`

Disadvantages
- A slight error in your coding can cost you heavily
- You have to master the parameters of the system to be able to do a thorough diagnosis should it malfunction

Backtesting tools

Each type of backtesting has its own tools that you can take advantage of:

Manual backtesting tools
- Forex Tester 2
- MetaTrader 4
- TradingView

With MetaTrader 4 and TradingView, you would need to use a spreadsheet program to track your trades. When it comes to analysis of your backtesting results, you can use the following tools:
- MetaTrader4 Reports
- Tradingrex
- Excel

Automated backtesting tools
- MetaTrader MLQ5
- TradingView (pine scripting language)
- TradeStation
- CandleScanner
- QuantShare

Stop Loss And Trailing Stop Loss

In this section, we will delve into more details about these very important risks management tools.

Stop loss

A stop-loss is an Order to buy or sell a forex currency once its price goes higher than or lower than a set stop price. Upon attaining the stop price, the stop order transforms into either a limit order (with a fixed or pre-determined price) or a market order (with no price limit). The stop order, once placed, is automatically triggered.

Without a price limit (market order, thus prevailing market price), the price at which the trade is executed may be different from that of the stop price (either higher or lower). This boosts chance of the trade being executed. However, at higher risk of selling lower than the stop price.

With a limit order, the trade must be executed at a certain pre-determined price or it lapses. This is because there could be lack of buyers or sellers willing to trade at the pre-determined price. It is less risky compared to a market order. However, it has lower chances of being executed compared to a market order.

Different kinds of Stop Loss Orders

1) Stop Loss Market Order

This is an order placed by a business entity to buy a security once its price goes higher than certain specified stop price or to sell a security once its price falls below the set stop price. In this regard, the trader has no control over the price at which the security will be sold. There are two types of Stop Loss Market Order:

- Sell Stop market order – This is an order placed by a seller to sell at the best market price after the price falls below the stop

price. It is an order to minimize losses when the seller suspects that the price is on a falling trend. Thus, the seller is able to sell a security before the price goes too low.
- A buy stop market order – This is an order placed by a buyer to buy at the best market price after the price rises above the stop price. It is an order to minimize losses when the buyer suspects that the prices are on a rising trend. Thus, the buyer is able to purchase a security before the price gets too high.

2) Stop Loss Limit Order

This is an order placed by a business entity to purchase a security at no more than or sell a security at no less than a certain fixed price (limit price). There are two types of stop-loss limit orders:
- Stop-loss buy limit order – This is an order placed by a buyer. It can only be executed at the limit price or lower.
- Stop loss sell limit order – This is an order placed by a seller, which gets transacted at the limit price or higher.

Trailing Stop Loss

A trailing stop-loss order, also known as trailing stop-on-quote order, is a stop order where the stop price automatically adjusts by a given point amount or a given percentage. Thus, the stop price automatically adjusts based on the last price of a security under consideration. For a sell order, the execution is triggered by the bid price, while, for buy orders, the execution is triggered by the ask price. Upon trigger by the stop price, a market order (to buy or sell) is sent to the market.

There are two types of trailing stop-loss orders:

- Trailing stop-loss sell order – When the difference between the security's last price and trigger price exceeds the trailing stop amount, then the trigger price is adjusted. The new trigger price will then be established by subtracting the trail stop amount from the security's last price.
- Trailing stop-loss buy order – When the difference between the security's last price and trigger price exceeds the trailing stop amount, then the trigger price get adjusted. The new trigger price will be established by

adding the trail stop amount to the last price.

Chapter 8   Trading the Breakout

Downside breakouts

The downside breakout, also known as the drop and stop, is a means of channel breakout trading that is particularly useful when used at the start of a specific session. It is a particularly useful strategy if you are set on trading the breakout and can't get anything else going at the moment. This means that the first thing you are going to want to watch out for is an evening star candlestick pattern which shows where the weekly pivot occurs.

An evening star candlestick pattern is a type of bearish pattern comprised of three distinct candles. The first is a large white candlestick that is found within the uptrend. The second will be red or white with a small body that closes above the first candle. Finally, the third candle will be large, red, and open underneath the second candle. It will also close near the center of the body of the first candle. If you see this pattern, then you can be confident the current uptrend is going to come to an end sooner than later.

After the price has made it through the upside breakout and then dropped into the downside breakout you were waiting for, it will then drop to a point that is lower than the weekly pivot point. This often leads to a number of price rejections before performing in such a way that it generates a rejection bar candle that is bearish which is a confirmation that the stop and drop is off to the races which means you can count on the price spiking downward to a significant degree.

While getting in once the confirmation has already happened will still generate a profit, it is going to be a situation that is far from ideal as the price is already headed towards the point where it will be exhausted. This means it will have a strong early upward movement, followed by a decline that is just as sharp. A majority of the average daily ranges will then have been used up at this point, something that the traders using this technique will be aware of. This means that if you want to use this strategy effectively you can't be afraid of a little micromanaging and also need to keep your expectations in check.

Furthermore, it is possible that there will not always be a visible rejection bar to make it easy to determine if the time is right. In these cases, you are going to want to use a polarity indicator to provide you with a better indication of when the market is moving in this direction. In a pinch, a number of bearish candles in a row that is growing increasingly severe as they move downward from the existing range. When any of these indicators occur, you should quickly determine the best entry point and do so using the next bearish candle by jumping in a few pips beneath the monthly pivot point.

Upside breakouts

If you find yourself in a situation where you are watching the price of one of your chosen currencies move into a tight range while at the same time waiting for what you believe to be a serious trend to start then the odds are high that by the time the price begins truly moving in earnest you will have already begun to miss out on profits that should be yours by right. Waiting to trade a breakout without preparing properly beforehand will often only lead to a scenario where rather than being ready for the breakout ahead of time you end up chasing the price which is a guaranteed means of minimizing profits at best or watching a winning trade turn into a losing one at worst.

Rejection bar candlestick: Many professional traders are extremely fond of the rejection bar candlestick, and with good reason, as it is one of the most useful technical analysis formations you can find.

It is a one bar formation that is known as the hammer or sometimes the inverted hammer forms when the currency has already rejected either the higher or the lower prices. This is visualized when a price opens before moving in a given direction and then reversing in the same session to close around or possibly just past the initial open. The best-case scenario then is one where both the close and the open of the rejection bar occur near one another, the closer the better.

Meanwhile, the tail of the bar needs to be a minimum of the same length as the body, with the longer tail typically indicating a stronger bar as it signifies that a low or high was previously rejected. The head of the bar is going to be the highest point of the price that was reached if the bar is bullish or the lowest if it is bearish. No matter how strong the bar appears to be, it should never be used as the sole justification for a given trade. As always, the more supplementary signals you have the better.

Specifically, if the price rejections can be tracked from a significant level, say the mid-level Bollinger band, then significant levels of resistance or support, or even a weekly pivot can tell you when you are onto a strong and reliable signal. Generally speaking, if you see a candlestick formation that starts to form by itself then the best course of action is going to be to look for additional reasons to enter the trade as they are going to be readily visible if the trade is worth pursuing.

Pop and stop: A pop and stop trade occurs when the price of the currency you are following suddenly pops out of the range it has been previously traveling in, stops temporarily and then resumes its previous movement. From this point on you will notice multiple rejection bars forming above and then rejecting nearby. If this then results in a larger than average candle you can realistically expect some retracement possibly enough for it to return to the previous range. This is due to the fact that the fast movement covered a sparse order area which can be seen via the gaps in the market. These gaps are naturally filled in by the market which means if you are going to get in then it needs to happen as quickly as possible.

Viable reasons for entering this type of trade include things like the time of day the pop occurred to begin with, especially if the price has been relatively quiet leading up to the beginning of the session when both volatility and liquidity are more likely to increase. This then often goes hand in hand with the price trading in a tight range. On the other hand, the price could previously move in a pop and stop motion, only to have formed rejection bars at previously relevant levels. If this occurs, then you will need to place a limit order that is a few pips lower or higher than the rejection bars. The stop loss will need to be placed just above or below the tail of the bars if you are an aggressive trader or below or above the highs or lows of the range if you are more conservative.

When you are looking for a pop and stop you are going to want to be aware of the fact that it is a relatively risky strategy. This is due to the fact that you are forced to rely on the gap created by the move to not be filled as quickly as what frequently occurs. The presence of rejection bars will also confirm the move to some extent but does not completely mitigate the potential for risk at the same time. The least risky time to use this strategy is when some time of news has just rocked the market. Once this happens you will have better luck trading in the direction the market sentiment is moving.

This will prove particularly useful if, prior to the news, the price was already trading at a particularly close range. It is important to keep an eye out for these types of announcements as they have the potential to reverse the sentiment and fill in the gap. You will need to be aware that this strategy requires a trend that is well supported in order to reach its full potential. This means that it is extremely important that you do your research beforehand in order to accurately determine if the session is likely to contain the level of liquidity that you are looking for in order to make this strategy into a profitable proposition. You will most frequently find the type of breakouts that you are looking for in open sessions of the forex market with London and New York being the prime candidates in most cases.

Additionally, it is important to maintain a level head when using this strategy and to never get greedy as the price movement after things take off can be substantial but is rarely prolonged. This is a strategy that relies on scalping, after all, which means that profits in the 1: 5: 1 or 2: 1 range are enough to bow out for.

NYSE Breakout Strategy

While this strategy only has a very specific use, it is worth keeping in mind as it can be quite profitable when executed on correctly. Using this strategy, you will want to be on the lookout for a breakout with a targeted resistance level to buy before waiting for a targeted support level to ultimately sell. This strategy works best with the

EUR/USD, USD/CHF, USD/JPY and GDP/USD currency pairs working from a 15 minute timeframe.

To best use this strategy, you will need to create a vertical line on the 15-minute chart for the currency pair you have chosen starting at 7 am EST and a second line at 9 am EST. From there you will need to create two horizontal lines at the highs of the various candles that appeared between the pair of vertical lines. From there, you will need to set a pending buy stop order that is between two and five pips above the current high point and a pending order to sell stop order that is a few points underneath the low. Finally, you will need to place a stop loss on the opposite end of each order as well.

With this done you will then be free to sit back and wait for the breakout to occur, which your research should have already indicated will not be that long. Once the breakout does occur you can then cancel the pending order you placed that is now useless as you will clearly not have to worry about it being activated. When everything is said and done you can often expect between

50 and 60 pips of profit from this strategy before most trends fizzle out.

Don't forget, when setting up this strategy you only have nine candlesticks to work with between 7 am and 9 am EST. As such, if the price doesn't appear to be trending either low or high then this is because the market is likely ranging. As such, you will most likely be better off canceling your orders as this strategy is only going to be effective if the right movement presents itself during this precise time period.

This is also known as a common time for various types of press releases to be released which means you are going to want to remain vigilant as your trade is in play to prevent anything unexpected happening without your knowledge. It is also important to keep in mind that if you start a trade based on GBP in the UK session then it can likely continue on into the US session in most cases.

The biggest advantage of this strategy is based on the fact that the way it is constructed virtually ensures that you can't overtrade, simply because you are only ever watching a single trade. As such, it is great for those without a lot of time or for those who aren't especially committed to trading and are just looking to try something out. Generally speaking, if you find a scenario where the difference between the highs and lows are less than 60 pips then be prepared to double your daily trade amount as this is a strong indicator that the forthcoming movement will be extremely profitable.

However, the downside of this strategy is that if the difference between the highs and lows is far greater than 60 pips then it is difficult for it to result in a profitable trade. This is due to the fact that price is unlikely to receive the required momentum to get it to where it would need to be in order to generate a profit for you. If things are setting up to fall this way, then you will want to aim for profit between 20 and 30 pips each day instead.

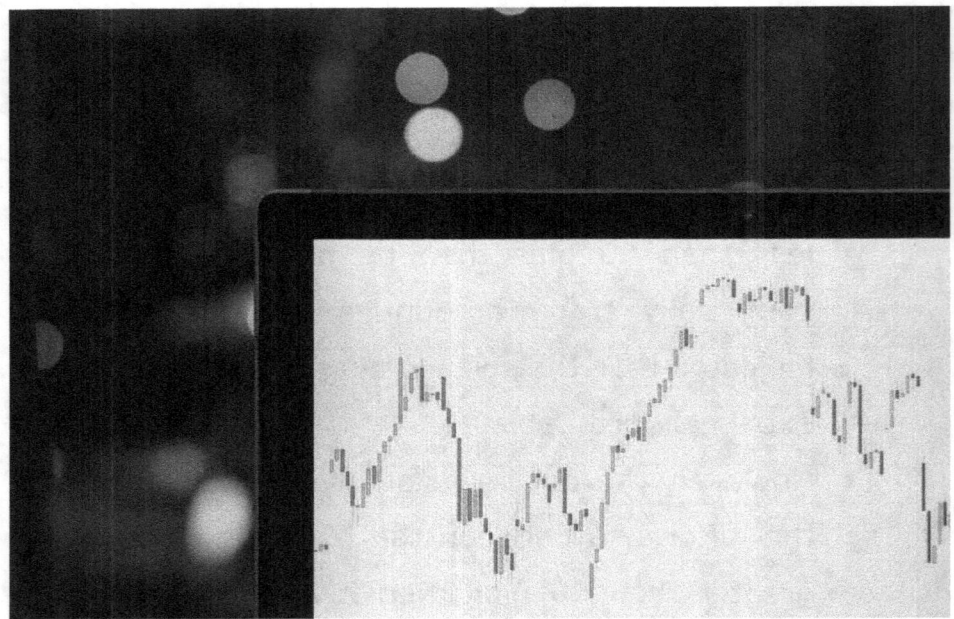

Chapter 9
Systems and Techniques for Beginners

Trading Systems

A trading system can be referred to as a group of parameters that are made specifically to determine the entry and exit of a trade of a given currency or security. As the parameters are used to do this, the determined points are frequently recorded and also marked in real-time to form a trend on a chart, and also trigger the execution of a trade immediately. This system saved the trader the hustle of using complicated procedure and therefore saves a lot of time. Again, because the system does all of the things and you are only give the final product, trading systems have saved traders from the use of their emotions in trading and can let other people do for them through a brokerage.

The systems, however, have their own limitations, regardless of its type. Most of these systems are more complex, and therefore, the traders need to know how parameters are used to make decisions the trader should also understand the technical analysis of the system to be able to use it. Therefore, before adopting a system for use in FOREX trade, take time to learn the systems so that you can know what to do with the trades and use the parameter presented on the chart on screens to make a trading decision.

In the trading world, everyone needs to know when to make an effective move, and the system you are using should not be a hindrance. To make sure that you understand the system completely, most traders use a custom made a system that is used for a particular trading strategy. For instance, a system for day trading might not be the same as the system for swing trading. A system that uses patterns a strategy for trading is not the best for use by traders who use fundamental strategies for trading. Therefore, as a trader you should know your best strategies and the skill you have, and choose a system that suits your strategies. Again, many systems can only work for a given period because the FOREX market is dynamic: it keeps on changing. The system you are using should be able to accommodate the changes through constant updates; otherwise, it becomes obsolete and cannot be used in the new trading markets.

Most traders have come up with systems that specialize in different trading strategies. For instance, when you are a trader that uses events that affect FOREX trading, you can use the Geopolitical turmoil trading system in your trades. There is always a microeconomic indicator to affect FX markets, for instance, most speeches made by governors, presidents, conferences prepared by the central bank of a country whose currency is in the FOREX market, and many others. These macroeconomic indicators are so powerful that they strike when least expected, and they are always unpredictable. The same case is on the geopolitical conflicts, which happens and surprises the traders because the changes that it brings to the market. Therefore if you choose to use the geopolitical trading system, make sure that you are ready to follow and monitor the events in the country of origin of the currencies you are pairing, so that you make a move that you are certain and it is beneficial. It is not advisable to wait for an event to happen for you to make a decision to buy either one of the currencies that you want to pair, always buy and have one of the currencies of your pair such that in case of an event that destabilizes the exchange of the paired currencies, you are always ready to act in your favor.

Another trading system is the use of candlestick patterns and moving averages. There are many variations in the moving averages, but the most popular one is the simple moving average, which is studying for a determined period. When using this system, the best thing to do is to find a moving average that is suitable for you, and then search for candlestick patterns that are around the moving average. It is therefore good to understand the candlestick patterns that might occur around a moving average and know when it is effective to employ them. The candlestick should also meet the criteria for higher success. As a beginner, before you use a candlestick and the simple moving average, always try the move using a demo account and practice until you perfect the skill, then use it in a real investment account.

Some people choose to use scalping as their trading strategy, and therefore, they can use this system for trading. The system requires that you generate trading signals using mostly the fundamental analysis; this is a manual system. There are automated systems, which does the analysis for you and gives you the signals on when to buy and when to sell. Automated trading can be best used by beginners, as they learn how to do it manually. However, the automated system deprives you of the possibility of gaining the skill; it is sometimes good to learn the hard way, but became better in trading. The skill helps you to have wide knowledge in analyzing and determining trade signals, remember that the FOREX market is volatile and the system can become obsolete unless it is constantly updated. There are systems that have been designed to do scalping using specific currency pair, and the most common is the USD/JPY EMA scalping strategy. The pair have been chosen because they are moderately volatile and also has moderate risk. This shows that everyone can develop their own trading system that works, provided that you do your research well. For example apart from the USD/JPY option, you can always choose your pair as long as they have characteristics that will help you manage trades without making loses.

The above-mentioned trading systems are not the only systems we have, there are many, and as said earlier, they depend on the trader's strategy. The only important thing to do is to know how to read the parameters affecting the trade of a particular currency, and know when they present a good entry point for entrance in the market and exit. As a beginner trader, invest your time in understanding your trading skills, then using your skills; choose your trading strategy, which will guide you on choosing the best trading system. Some trading systems require your attention all the time, and this aspect should be considered when determining the system to use.

Trading Techniques for Beginners

FOREX market is the largest in the financial market around the globe. It has different techniques for trading, which involves the selling and buying securities of stocks, softs, indices, and metals, among others and currencies. The techniques use different systems and platforms that ensure that trading activities are executed effectively. Those who use different techniques use different strategies, as they speculate and predict what is the best move to maximize profits. The four basic techniques used are day trading, swing trading, position trading, and scalp trading.

Use the Day Trading techniques

Day trading is a technique where a trade opens trading positions and after trading with them, he or she closes all of them; at the point of closure of the trading day, no trades are open. This type of trading requires that the trader has experience and extensive knowledge on what constitutes FOREX trading and it is done. Before a day trader makes a decision, he or she employs different strategies that will guide him or her on the best strategies for success. Traders sometimes use technical indicators to make and do calculations on the time frames where exit and entry are favorable. Others use their instincts to make a decision on the best move that will yield profits. The traders that use this technique use the price action characteristics to hold position, and to trade currencies; they rarely use fundamental information. Traders only concentrate on the volatility of the currency and day range; a trade is only initiated if there is enough price movement because day traders realize their profits through price movements of the selected currency. The trader establishes a trade by moving in the trade and leaving the trade very fast, and therefore, the liquidity and volume of currency traded are important aspects of this technique of trading. This means that traders concentrate only on the currencies with a large volume and daily range. The events that will have a short term effect on the price and volume of currencies are appreciated much by day traders. For example news on certain economic aspects makes day trading good for many traders; these aspects include interest rates, release of information on the corporate earnings and economic statistics.

Use the Position Trading technique

Position trading in the FOREX market involves holding or taking a trade position longer. The period can be as long as years, months and as short as weeks. Traders that use this technique do not care much about the price fluctuation of currencies in the short terms and the daily news release. The technique does not make the trader active, because he or she can make very few positions for a whole year. They utilize the weekly or monthly price action chart analysis to determine security moves towards a given trend, and therefore, they use primary trends to make their profits. Unlike in the day trading technique, position technique uses technical and fundamental indicators analysis, which gives the trader a good look at the FOREX market before they make decisions.

Implement the Swing Trading techniques

It is a trading technique that is used by traders to make profits through taking a trading position overnight that goes for a few weeks the traders that utilize. This strategy mostly uses fundamental indicators analysis, which includes analysis of patterns, the intrinsic value of the traded currency, trends in the prices of the currency. They also use technical analysis to find short terms momentum price. The traders look for a currency that would have an extraordinary move within a short time frame. They are interested in trading with large price changes in a day, which prompts them to spend weeks or even months monitoring to find the large price move. When the price suddenly swings in the upwards direction, these traders trade their currencies by selling and when there is a halt in the swing, the traders stop selling, or they would have already left the trade. The focus on given assets help them to understand its movement, and its advantage lies in the huge returns by the traders; which is contrary to investors who buy and hold. This technique in trading can be used by traders in earning a living, as they have fewer risks compared to other trading techniques. In addition, the trader does not need to be checking real-time data and analyzing it to determine when to make a move that makes profits. The people who engage in part-time trading can use this technique as it does not need full-time commitment.

Employ the Scalp Trading

This is a type of trading where a trader trades currencies and holds on the position only for a short time, hoping that within the short time of hold he or she will get an opportunity to take another trading position bringing in profits. The traders take several positions in a day with the hope that that within the day, they would make a considerable amount from several small percentage profits in the market. To maximize on opportunities that show up in the market for a short time, the trader develops functional trading strategies such as the use of hotkeys to make desirable executions at the computer. On the other hand, those using the automated trading system uses set rules and guidelines to determine a trade signal.

In FOREX trading, traders make huge profits, but it is a market that is full of risks. It is therefore important for the trader to analyze his or her trading skills, and choose wisely whether he or she wants to be a swing trader, day trader, scalping trader, or position trader.

Conclusion

Figuring out how to exchange Forex effectively can be entangled for learners. A great many people need to get rich medium-term, regardless of how unreasonable it might sound. The universe of Forex trading can be a touch of overpowering, particularly in the event that you are new to the game, and don't have a clue about the standards yet. You have to plunge your toes in before you go any more profound. Fortunately, we have your back! We've aggregated a rundown of 20 Forex tips for apprentices to help you along your trading venture 2020. In the event that you as of now have involvement with Forex trading, it's in every case great to recall the nuts and bolts.

1. Pick Your Broker Wisely

Picking the correct agent is a large portion of the fight. Take as much time as is needed to check surveys and suggestions. Ensure the agent you pick is dependable and suits your trading character. Keep in mind, there are heaps of phony dealers out there who will just hold you up. Go for an approved intermediary with a permit.

2. Make Your Own Strategy

No rundown of cash trading tips is finished in the event that it doesn't make reference to systems. One of the most widely recognized errors novice dealers make isn't making an activity plan. Make sense of what you need to escape trading. Having an unmistakable ultimate objective as a top priority will help with your trading discipline.

3. Learn Step-by-Step

Similarly as with each new useful learning action, trading expects you to begin with the nuts and bolts, and move gradually until you comprehend the playing field. Start by contributing little totals of cash, and remember the familiar proverb 'moderate however consistent successes the race'.

4. Assume Responsibility for Your Emotions

Try not to give your feelings a chance to divert you. It tends to be troublesome now and again, particularly after you've encountered a losing streak. Be that as it may, keeping a level head will enable you to remain reasonable, so you can settle on equipped decisions. At whatever point you let your feelings improve of you, you open yourself to superfluous dangers. Practicing risks the executives inside your trading will assist you with minimizing the dangers.

5. Stress Less

This is one evident Forex tip – in light of the fact that it is. Be that as it may, prepare to have your mind blown. Trading under pressure for the most part prompts unreasonable choices, and in live trading, that will cost you cash. In this manner, recognize the wellspring of your pressure and attempt to dispense with it, or possibly limit its effect on you. Take a full breath and spotlight on something different. Each individual has their method for conquering pressure – some tune in to old style music, while others work out. Tune in to your emotional wellness and realize what works best for you.

6. Careful discipline brings about promising results

Of all the Forex deceives and tips for novices, this is the most significant. You are probably not going to prevail at anything on your first attempt. Just steady trading practice can yield reliably top outcomes. Be that as it may, you most likely would prefer not to lose cash while learning the rudiments. Fortunately for you, trading on a demo account costs nothing to liberate up and is to utilize!

7. Brain research is Key

Each merchant is a therapist on the most fundamental level. At the point when you're arranging your best course of action, you need to dissect showcase developments and audit your own brain science. You have to ask yourself inquiries, for example,

- Did I give indications of affirmation inclination?
- Did I make an exchange out of dissatisfaction?
- What caused me to pick that specific money pair?

Acing your brain science will shield you from numerous misfortunes along the trading advancement way.

8. No Risk, No Success

Not even Forex trading tips and deceives can promise you achievement. At the point when you choose to turn into a broker, you ought to have just acknowledged the plausibility of disappointment. In the event that you didn't – here's a rude awakening. You won't make productive exchanges 100% of the time. Try not to give false commercials a chance to get in your mind, either. Rather, be practical about your Forex trading techniques and objectives.

www.ingramcontent.com/pod-product-compliance
Lightning Source LLC
Chambersburg PA
CBHW070632220526
45466CB00001B/156